SALES AND DISTRIBUTION MANAGEMENT

RUPA RATHEE, PhD
Associate Professor
Department of Management Studies
Deenbandhu Chhotu Ram University of Science and Technology (DCRUST)
Murthal, Haryana

PALLAVI RAJAIN, PhD
Assistant Professor
Department of Management
Maharaja Surajmal Institute
Janakpuri, New Delhi

PHI Learning Private Limited
Delhi-110092
2024

₹ 595.00

SALES AND DISTRIBUTION MANAGEMENT
Rupa Rathee and Pallavi Rajain

ISBN-978-93-91818-73-9 (Print Book)
ISBN-978-93-91818-77-7 (e-Book)

The export rights of this book are vested solely with the publisher.

Published by Asoke K. Ghosh, PHI Learning Private Limited, Rimjhim House, 111, Patparganj Industrial Estate, Delhi-110092 and Printed by Multi Colour Services, I-45, DLF Industrial Area, Sector-32, Faridabad, Haryana-121003.

Dedicated to

My loving husband Mr. Tejinder Rathee and doting daughter
Ms. Anvika and all family members for their love and support.

—Dr. Rupa Rathee

My parents Maj. YS Rajain and Mrs. Manju Rajain
for their blessings and brother Aakash for his encouragement.

—Dr. Pallavi Rajain

Contents

Preface

This book has been written due to the authors' interest in the field of Marketing. The world has changed in its approach of selling goods and services. As such marketers need to focus on more than just the qualities of the products. Thus, a need was felt by the authors to focus on the topic of Sales and Distribution Management.

The main purpose of this book is to provide a detailed insight of various aspects of sales and distribution management to its readers with a thorough coverage supported with, case studies and examples. For convenience and ease of understanding, the book is divided into two sections:

Chapter 1 discusses the definition, nature, scope and objectives of sales management along with the responsibilities of sales management. The chapter also focuses on certain emerging trends in sales management.

Chapter 2 deals with the various theories of selling like "AIDAS" Theory of Selling, "Right Set of Circumstances" Theory of Selling, "Buying Formula" Theory of Selling, "Behavioural Equation" Theory and Modern Approaches of Sales.

Chapter 3 deals with the process of personal selling in a logical sequence of Prospecting, Preparation, Presentation, Handling Objections, Closing and Follow-up.

Chapter 4 explores the strategic salesforce planning, sales forecasting and budgeting of the sales management.

Chapter 5 deals with the purpose of sales organisation. Further, the role of sales administration and types of sales organisation structures are discussed.

Chapter 6 is about management of sales quotas and territories. It discusses the administration of quota system and the limitations associated with it. Next, the procedure for territory formation is discussed along with the criteria for territory formation. Lastly, various territory shapes and different ways of dealing with territory management problem are provided.

Chapter 7 elaborates on staffing of salesforce.

Chapter 8 describes the aims, contents, methods of training, execution and evaluation (ACMEE) of the salesforce.

Chapter 9 discusses motivational needs of the salesforce and the different theories of motivation.

Chapter 10 deals with requirements of a good sales compensation plan. Also, it describes various sales compensation plans, besides the use of bonus and fringe benefits.

Chapter 11 is about controlling the salesforce by using sales audit and market share analysis. Next, it discusses the concepts of salesforce automation and social selling through social media.

Chapter 12 is on managing the international salesforce and issues related to international sales and marketing.

Chapter 13 deals with managing sales during crises.

Chapter 14, which is a part of the second section of the book, begins with an introduction to the basic concepts of distribution management.

Chapter 15 deals with the designing of marketing channels. It also discusses channel levels, channel flows, prominent channel systems, kinds of channel members, distribution policies and strategies and special distribution methods.

Chapter 16 and Chapter 17 are focused on the channel institutions that is retailing and wholesaling.

Chapter 18 describes the designing of channel systems.

Chapter 19 deals with the channel management, evaluation and control where power bases, channel conflict and channel coordination are discussed.

Chapter 20 discusses the digital supply networks. In this chapter mainly the short-term and long-term risk management strategies associated with distribution are discussed.

The last but not least Chapter 21 deals with logistics and supply chain management, and also, differentiates between the two. It also discusses various aspects related to inventory management, warehousing and different modes of transport.

Rupa Rathee
Pallavi Rajain

Acknowledgements

The authors would like to thank the Department of Management Studies, Deenbandhu Chhotu Ram University of Science and Technology where most of the research has been done. The Department provided the necessary resources in completing the research for this book.

Special thanks to Honourable Vice-Chancellor Dr. Rajender Kumar Anayath, Deenbandhu Chhotu Ram University of Science and Technology for continually being a source of inspiration. His vision for to take the University to new era of digitisation and globalisation through latest trends has inspired the thoughts of many.

Many thanks to Prof Anil Khurana, Chairman, Department of Management Studies, Deenbandhu Chhotu Ram University of Science and Technology for his encouragement and stimulation to achieve new heights. He constantly provokes members of the department to make innovative contributions in the field of academics and research.

The authors would like to thank the editors of PHI Learning for publishing this book. The editorial team greatly helped in smoothing the editing and publishing process.

Finally, the authors would like to thank their families and friends for their continuous support during this project. It would not have been possible to complete this text without their unwavering support.

Rupa Rathee
Pallavi Rajain

SECTION 1
SALES MANAGEMENT

1

Sales Management
An Introduction

LEARNING OBJECTIVES

LO1: To understand definition, nature and scope of sales management

LO2: To explain the objectives of sales management

LO3: To describe responsibilities of sales management

LO4: To discuss the levels of sales management

LO5: To identify emerging trends in sales management

INTRODUCTION

In earlier times, before the industrial revolution, most of the focus was on manufacturing as the industries were small scale. Post industrial revolution, when industries began to expand the departments were segregated and each department separate was allocated different task. It is at this time that a separate sales department came into existence. The department has an important position as it has an income generating function.

DEFINITIONS

It is the planning, direction and control of personal selling, including recruiting, selecting, equipping, assigning, supervising, paying and motivating as these tasks apply to the personal salesforce.

— American Marketing Association

It is also defined as "Sales Management includes recruiting, selecting, training, supervising, motivating and evaluating the sales-force."

—Rachman and Romano.

Sales Management is primarily the direction of men with all the management functions, of organisation, control, recruitment, training, supervision and motivation.

—Hampton and Zabin.

Sales Management is the part of the management in which the aim of an organisation is to make provision for the sale of the produced commodities.

—Hain- R. Tosdal.

Sales Management involves the direction and control of salesmen, sales planning, budgeting, policy making, coordination of marketing research, advertising, sales promotion and merchandising and the integration in the marketing programme of all business activities that contribute to the increased sales and profits.

— B.R. Canfield

NATURE OF SALES MANAGEMENT

Today sales management includes, major activities like recruiting and selecting a salesforce, and then training, supervising and motivating these people.

Figure 1.1 Nature of Sales Management

Goal Oriented: Like other administrative exercises, sale is conducted for a particular reason and expected for the accomplishment of objectives or targets.

Continuous Process: The salesforce requires to perform sales activities with the other tasks in routine and this cycle is ever going.

Systematic Approach: It is a coordinated approach to dealing with the business capability of the organisation where each problem has a characterised and demonstrated arrangement.

Relationship Selling: The salesmen attempts to develop strong relationship with their customers.

Marketing Management Integration: Sales Management is integrated with the other Ps of marketing like product, price, place and promotion (for example, sales promotion, advertising, etc.).

Different Sales or Job Position: It is a joint effort of the entire sales team including sales representative, sales leader, sales head, project supervisor, etc.

Pervasive Function: It is an essential activity performed by all types of business organizations.

SCOPE OF SALES MANAGEMENT

Earlier sales management had a narrow scope involving activities such as motivating, training, selecting and recruiting. However, in present times the scope is much broader. It includes the following:

Sales Planning or Forecasting: Through anticipation of future sales prospective there is a need to plan the sales-related activities well in advance.

Sales Budgeting: In carrying out the sales activities some expenses will be incurred as estimated or determined through the sales budget prepared by the sales manager.

Determining Structure and Size of Sales Organisation: Sales organisation is the department of a company which is solely responsible for all functions that are sales-related.

The structure, composition and size of a sales organisation are determined by sales management.

Human Resource Planning: A correct estimate of sales personnel requirement in the organisation is ensured through sales management.

Hiring Sales Personnel: Various vacant sales positions are filled by initiating the recruitment and selection of suitable and efficient candidates.

Development and Training of Salespeople: It also includes providing orientation and training to the candidates that have been selected so as to develop their knowledge and skills to match those required for the job position.

Developing Salesperson's Objectives: For the salespeople appointed under him/her, the sales manager can set up achievable goals or objectives.

Fixing Sales Quotas: Also, to set targets for the sales team the sales quota (yearly, quarterly or monthly) is fixed, either in terms of value of sales or volume.

Determining Sales Territories: Every sales team or salesperson needs to penetrate a particular region or area for selling products or services as a target market.

Motivating Sales Personnel: It also emphasises on better performance of salespersons and reviewing the work of salespeople.

Compensation and Remuneration of Salespeople: It ascertains appropriate commission, allowance, remuneration, salary and other benefits to the salespeople.

Controlling Salesforce: To monitor the performance of the sales personnel who exercise sufficient control is also a crucial function of sales management.

Branding, Labelling and Packaging: Customer feedback on the acceptability of the product packaging presentation, branding and labelling is gathered by the sales personnel.

Managing Distribution Channel: It also ensures keeping track of the marketing channels and filling the loopholes, if any.

Sales Promotion: Through sales management functions, the product advertisements and other promotional tactics are also determined.

Organising and Support Service: Through proper guidance and support service handling of queries and solving problems of the sales personnel is done.

After-Sale Services: The concern of sales management is the customer who recognises a company mostly through the efficiency and effectiveness of the after-sale services it provides.

OBJECTIVES OF SALES MANAGEMENT

The general objectives of sales management are divided into three:

- Continuing growth
- Contribution to profits
- Sales volume

It is often observed that sales executives make major contributions even if they do not carry the full burden in the effort to meet the above objectives.

Often by breaking down objectives and restating as definite goals they get translated into more specific goals. Goal setting is preceded by planning. In planning, sales executives provide estimates on the capabilities of the sales force and middlemen; sales potentials and market.

In charting the course of future operations, sales management is instrumental. The activity provides top management with informed estimates and facts for setting sales and profit goals and making marketing decisions. The financial results and sales management of a company are related.

The net profit of a company is influenced by sales, gross margin and expenses which are influenced by the performance of sales management. How sales are being managed within a company are not directly affected by the cost of sales. Maintenance of targeted unit costs of production and distribution can be indirectly affected since sales volume must be large enough.

Some Other Objectives of Sales Management

1. **Revenue Generation:** To generate revenue for the organisation is one of the main objectives of sales management. The sole responsibility of bringing in the money is with the sales department.

2. **Increase Sales Volume:** The organisation wishes to increase the number of units sold through efficient sales management. This ensures that the production facilities do not remain idle and have full utilisation.

3. **Sustained Profits:** Sales management has an objective of improving the profits of the organisation through effective control, coordination and planning. To ensure good profits for the organisation, sales management strives to reduce costs and increase sales.

4. **Organisation Growth:** For the growth of the organisation there is a need of continuous and sustained sales management techniques so that the organisation tends to gain market share and results.

5. **Market Leadership:** 'Sales management' enables an organisation to become the market leader with increased profits and sales volumes.

6. **Converting Prospects to Customers:** Sustained efforts and good planning are required for connecting prospects with customers. This is accomplished through sales management.

7. **Motivate the Sales Force:** Motivating the salesforce is one of the core objectives of sales management. Achieving sales targets can become very challenging as selling is a very stressful task. Therefore, continuous motivation through reward systems and proper incentives is the sales management task.

8. **Compliment Marketing Activities:** Supporting marketing functions of the organisation is the sales management's task. To achieve the desired results, marketing and sales need to go hand in hand.

The three major objectives the sales function is expected to achieve are sales volume, contribution to profits and growth. Sales contribute a great deal in achieving them even though these are broad corporate functions to be achieved by the top management. Corporate objectives are communicated to the marketing department which in turn passes on the responsibility to the sales department.

SALES MANAGEMENT RESPONSIBILITIES

A crucial role is played by the sales manager in the success or failure of an organisation. The task of generating revenue and achieving sales target is mainly the responsibility of a sales manager. If one of these activities is performed poorly, it will have a ripple effect on the others.

I. Primary Responsibility of a Sales Manager

The primary responsibility of a sales manager is to staff the organisation with the right people.

Good selection is particularly important in sales management because marketing is an art of implementation.

Figure 1.2 Sales Manager (*Source:* Wikimedia Commons)

II. Role and Skills of a Sales Manager

Roles: *Changing Roles*

♦ Fostering a more point by point comprehension of client's business.

♦ Regarding sales reps as equivalents and working in organisation with them to accomplish benefit and consumer loyalty.

♦ Applying adaptable persuasive devices to a mixture deals power of Telesellers, direct advertisers and field sales reps.

♦ Staying up with the latest on the most recent advancements influencing purchaser vender connections.

♦ Working intimately with other interior divisions as an individual from the corporate group trying to accomplish consumer loyalty.

♦ Ceaselessly looking for ways of surpassing client assumptions and carry enhanced the purchaser dealer relationship.

♦ Establishing an adaptable learning and adjusting climate.

Skills

♦ They must be sensitive to individual needs and skills.

♦ They must emphasise more on communicating and coaching than monitoring and controlling.

♦ They must possess the ability of analysing and interpreting facts correctly.

♦ They must be efficiently able to structure different departments in an organisation.

III. Sales Managers are Administrators

A sales manager is first and foremost a manager—an administrator and management is a distinct skill.

♦ Sales ability is not enough—The sales talent alone does not make a good manager

♦ He has to frame the sales plan and policies of the organisation. He is also responsible for the coordination of activities between departments.

IV. Sales Managers' Job Differs from Other Managerial Jobs

Sales managers and other managers both supervise groups of employees but play different roles in their occupation.

Sales managers are responsible for managing the employees in charge of selling a product or service, while other managers focus on gauging the demand for these goods.

Sales managers and other managers both work to supply customers with a product or service but in very different ways. Other managers just oversee strategies for getting new products and services to potential customers.

Sales managers use data and training in an effort to better equip sales associates to reach their department's sales goals.

Both types of managers focus on analysing sales projections and the market.

LEVELS OF SALES MANAGEMENT

Top-level Sales Executives

The highest executive in sales management is most often called Vice-President of Sales. He reports to the vice-president/ head of marketing or to the President directly. These people are responsible for controlling the performance, implementing action plans and strategies, setting short-term and long-term objectives, developing strategies to achieve them, scanning external environment, marketing and sales planning.

Middle-level Sales Executives

♦ These positions usually carry the title of regional or divisional sales manager.

♦ He is responsible for managing several sales districts.

♦ Sometimes the job title is branch manager, especially when the branch office carries product inventory and performs physical distribution activities.

Figure 1.3   Levels of Sales Management

First-level Sales Executives

Sales supervisor is an entry-level position of sales management.

Usually in a limited geographical area they provide day-to-day training, advice and supervision for a small number of salespeople (usually part of a sales district).

The next position is district sales manager, who manages the activities of sales supervisors or team leaders and participates in some sales planning and evaluation activities in the district.

SALES MANAGEMENT: EMERGING TRENDS

Customer Orientation

Retaining customers for a long period, delivering more satisfaction to them and giving them high value services is possible through processes, systems and structures designed around customers.

Relationship Selling

Long-term relationships need to be developed by the sales staff with customers which is a part of relationship selling strategy. These relationships need to be built across the organisation for the different kinds of staff. Loyalty programmes of airline companies such as Jet Airways are a good example.

Technology

It has a two-way impact in terms of selling function as well as its performance. Automation of salesforce has been possible because of new technology. The demand pattern of customers could be studied with the help of technology. This has reduced the role of the salesperson as an order taker. For example, the Gurgaon plant of Maruti has an automated sales process where the demand patterns are linked to the production of different types of cars.

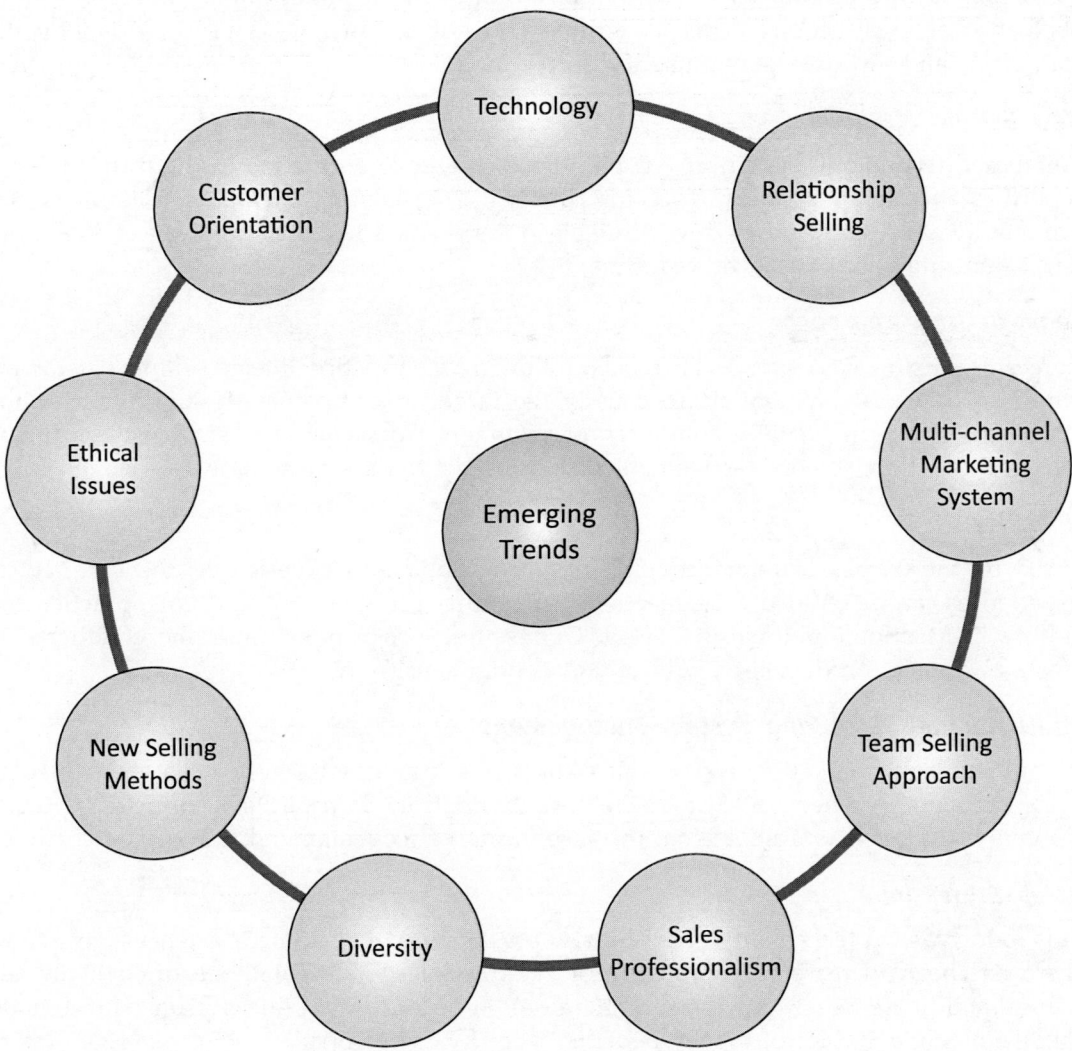

Figure 1.4 Emerging Trends

Ethical Issues

The business decisions of different countries are governed by various legislations in these countries. So, salespeople are posed with challenges as business practices are guided by ethics of those countries. Bribery, deception and high pressure of sales tactics are faced by the salespeople. In order to get an order, giving a gift or payment is misleading as it exaggerates the benefits of the product and using high-pressure sales tactics of committing wrong delivery schedules to customers in need of urgent deliveries are examples of unethical behaviour. Ethical standards need to be ensured by the sales managers as they may end up in legal problems or loss of business. Adherence to social responsibility includes participation in community development programs, satisfaction of public expectations and obedience of legal requirements. A written code of conduct must be provided by the companies and top managers must act as role models.

New Selling Methods

Web-based technology has improved the virtual presence on the job in the form of faster reporting and better availability of information. The emergent wireless technology has brought another world order in which wait-in periods are taken, supply cycles, inventory levels and quotations based on real-time.

Team Selling Approach

In recent years most companies have been following the practice of team selling. Customers who have high sales potential are usually the target of companies through team selling approach. The team usually composes of members from customer service department, technical function, senior management and manufacturer's representatives.

Diversity

Based on the frames of reference, culture, background and experiences; the diversity of experiences can be defined. Organisations must approach diversity in rituals, practice and culture in a serious and sensitive way. Counselling programmes must be conducted to create awareness on disability, culture and gender sensitivity.

Multi-channel Marketing System Management

A multi-channel marketing system, also known as hybrid sales system, is used to reach more than one segment of customers through multiple distribution channels. Its major benefits include customised selling, increase in market coverage and low cost of channels.

Sales Professionalism

Due to increase in technicality of services, sophistication of customers, intense competition there has been increase in complexity of selling. Salespersons with acquired skills and natural ability are usually successful. Therefore, in order to train salespersons and to make them professional, a lot of money is being spent by the companies.

CASE STUDY

Shivam Sinha, Manager, Shaan Products Ltd., lay in bed at the company's Mumbai guest house. Shivam came to Mumbai from Delhi on transfer 10 days earlier. Around a month back, Shivam was called by General Manager, Ajay Rastogi, in Delhi. He said "Shivam you have been performing very well as the branch manager, Delhi. The management has, therefore, decided to promote you to the next position of regional sales manager of Western Region. Many congratulations to you." After a warm handshake with Ajay Rastogi, Shivam replied, "Sir, many thanks for the promotion and the recognition of my efforts, but why am I transferred to the Western region of all the four regions?" Ajay smiled and said, "Well, basically to set things right! You see, the company has not been performing well in the Western region in terms of sales and profits for the past three years. We thought that with your managerial abilities you can make a positive change in the performance of the Western region, and hence this transfer from Delhi to Mumbai." All these matters came to Shivam's mind while lying in the bed.

Shaan Products Ltd. has been manufacturing and marketing consumer durable products such as fans and lighting since 1980. The company has three manufacturing units in Delhi, Hyderabad and Ludhiana. It is headquartered in Delhi. The company is managed professionally. It has two divisions. Fan division manufactures exhaust, pedestal, wall, table and ceiling fans. The lighting division produces consumer lighting products such as LED and CFL lamps, lighting accessories, gate lighting and home décor lighting. The company's products are known for quality. It has a good relationship with dealers and distributors and a strong distribution network.

Shivam had completed his MBA from a top management institute, after obtaining a degree in commerce. He understood that his role as a regional sales manager would be different from his previous position. In Delhi, as a branch manager, salespeople were reporting to him. He was directly responsible to manage salespeople and achieve the goals in terms of profit contribution, market share and sales for the branch. But now, as a regional sales manager, he is expected to manage the branches of Western region viz. Mumbai, Surat, Goa and Pune. He will be responsible for achieving profit contribution targets, customer satisfaction, market share and sales for Western region through the branch managers. In addition, Shivam will be responsible for allocating eastern sales and expenditure budgets to the four branches, organising training programmes for salespeople and support staff, coordinating with sales promotion and advertising agencies, reviewing branch performance every month and discussing and deciding corrective actions to be taken.

Shivam thought that he was clear about his role and the tasks to be performed as a regional sales manager. However, he wondered what management concepts and techniques should he use to set things right, so that the performance of Western region improves to the expectations of the management.

Question

1. If you were Shivam Sinha, what would you do and why?

SUMMARY

Sales Management is the management of the personal-selling component of an organisation's marketing programme. The three major objectives the sales role is expected to achieve are Sales volume, contribution to profits and growth. Sales contribute a great deal in achieving them even though these are broad corporate functions to be achieved by the top management. Corporate objectives are communicated to the marketing department who in turn passes on the responsibility to the sales department. There are several responsibilities of a sales manager. The primary responsibility of a sales manager is to staff the organisation with the right people. There are various types of sales managers like national sales manager, regional sales manager and district sales manager working at different levels in an organisation like top level and middle level positions. Lastly, the emerging trends are discussed which include customer orientation, technology, relationship selling, diversity, new selling methods and ethical issues.

KEY TERMS

Selling concept: It proposes that customers will not buy enough of an organisation's products unless they are persuaded to do so through selling efforts.

Sales management: It is the planning, direction and control of personal selling, including recruiting, selecting, equipping, assigning, supervising, paying and motivating as these tasks apply to the personal salesforce.

Sales manager: A sales manager is a manager responsible for the sales in a store, including the supervision of sales associates and other employees in a particular geographic region.

Relationship selling: It is the sales technique that focuses on the interaction between the buyer and the sales person, rather than the price or details of the product.

Team selling: It is a sales strategy commonly used in account-based selling to close more deals.

EXERCISES

1.1 Define sales management along with its nature and scope.

1.2 What are the objectives of sales management?

1.3 What are the sales management responsibilities?

1.4 What are the various levels of sales management?

1.5 List some of the contemporary issues in sales management.

2

Theories of Selling

LEARNING OBJECTIVES

LO1: To learn about AIDAS theory of selling

LO2: To understand the Right set of circumstances theory

LO3: To learn about Buying-formula theory of selling

LO4: To understand Behavioural equation theory

LO5: To learn about the modern approaches to sale

INTRODUCTION

There are two contrasting approaches related to the theory of selling because of the fact that selling is considered as a science by some and art by others. The first approach was related to gaining experience from successful salespeople as well as professionals in advertising. These people succeeded in their fields due to their practical application of knowledge gained through experiences. These theories stress on the "how" and "what" rather than "why". The second approach was based on the findings of behavioural scientists. The psychologists in this field tried to develop a unified theory of buying and selling.

There are four important theories:

(i) AIDAS theory
(ii) Right set of circumstances theory
(iii) Buying-formula theory of selling
(iv) Behavioural equation theory

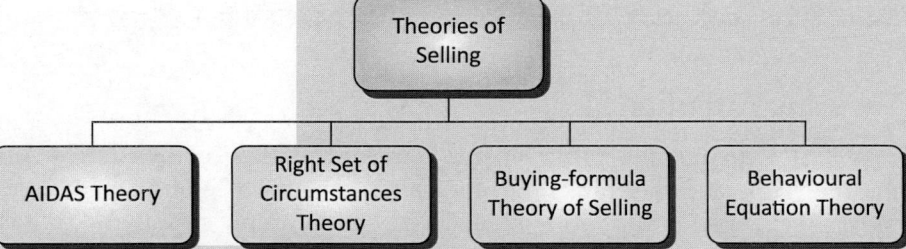

Figure 2.1 Theories of Selling

AIDAS THEORY OF SELLING

According to this theory, given by Elmo Lewis, the prospect's mind passes through five successive mental states, during the successful selling interview:

A	Attention
I	Interest
D	Desire
A	Action
S	Satisfaction

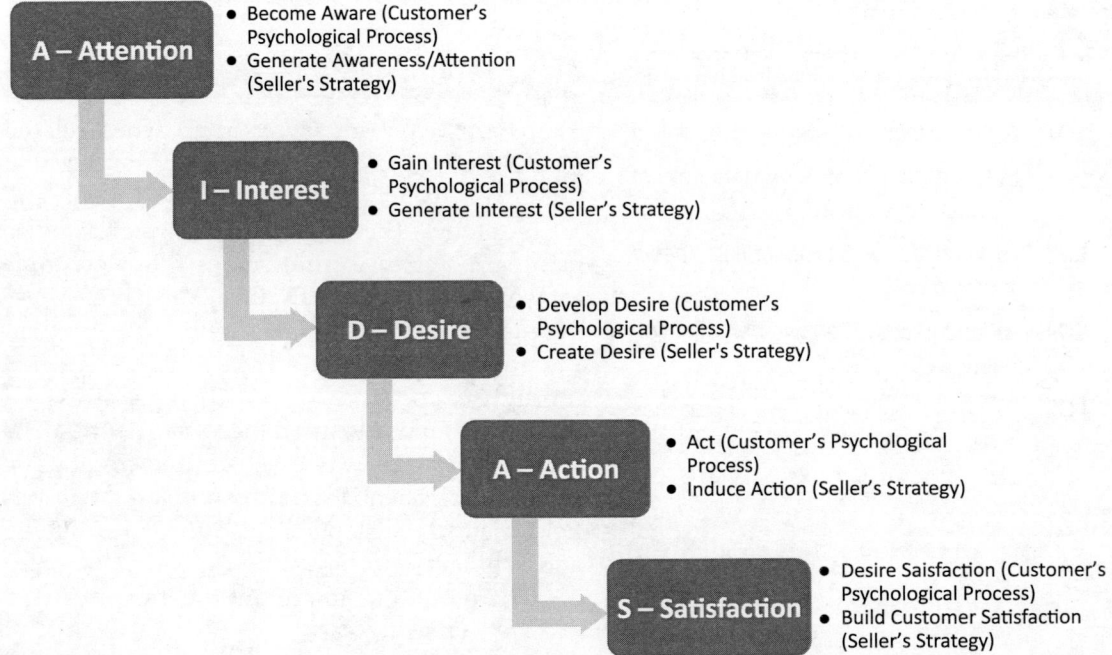

Figure 2.2 AIDAS Theory of Selling

The prospect goes through these five stages consciously, so the sales presentation must lead the prospect through them in the right sequence if a sale is to result.

Securing Attention

The goal is to put the prospect into a receptive state of mind. The prospects guard is naturally up, since he thinks that the caller is bent on selling something. The salesperson must establish good rapport at once. He needs an ample supply of "conversation openers".

First impression must be favourable, there should be proper attire, neatness, friendliness and genuine smile. Conversation openers should be avoided if they cannot be linked to the rest of the presentation as the conversation may wander off making it difficult to return to the original theme.

It is advantageous if the opening remarks are about:

♦ Prospect

♦ Prospect's business (favourable comment)

Gaining Interest

The second goal is to intensify the prospect's attention so that it evolves into strong interest. Many techniques are used to gain interest. Some salespeople develop a contagious enthusiasm for the product or a sample. If the product is bulky, portfolio or other visual aids can be used. In this phase the salesperson hopes to find what is most likely to appeal to a prospect. The prospect may even drop hints which help the salesperson in selecting the best approach that should be adopted.

Prospect's interests are affected by:

♦ Basic motivations.

♦ Closeness of the interview subjects to current problems.

♦ Timeliness.

♦ Their mood—receptive, sceptical or hostile.

The salesperson must take all these into account in selecting the appeal to emphasise.

Kindling Desire

The third goal is to kindle the prospect's desire to the ready-to-buy point. The salesperson must keep the conversation running along the mainline towards the sale. The development of sales obstacles, the prospect's objections, external interruptions can side-track the presentation during this phase. Satisfactory answers must be provided for objections. If the objections are anticipated and answered before a prospect raises them then, there are better chances of making a sale. All these must be handled tactfully.

Inducing Actions

If the presentation has been perfect, the prospect is ready to i.e., to buy. Buying is not automatic, as a rule, it must be induced. Salesperson must close a deal at the right time. The trial close, the close on a minor point, and the trick close are used to test the prospect's reaction. Any technique should be used so that an action takes place. Salesperson may not ask for a definite "yes" or "no" for the fear of rejection but it is always better to ask for a straightforward answer.

Building Satisfaction

After the customer has given the order, the salesperson should reassure the customer that the decision was correct. Building satisfaction means:

◆ Thanking the customer for the order.

◆ Attending to such matters as making certain that the order is filled as written.

◆ Following up on promises made.

"RIGHT SET OF CIRCUMSTANCES" THEORY OF SELLING

It is also called the "situation-response" theory. The particular circumstances prevailing in a given selling situation cause the prospect to respond in a predictable way. More skilled the salesperson is in handling the set of circumstances, the more predictable is the response. The set of circumstances, includes external or internal to the prospect. A minimum of four factors has an effect on the response. This includes the presence or absence of desires:

(i) Having a cup of coffee.

(ii) Having it at the moment.

(iii) Going out now or not at all.

(iv) Going out with the salesperson.

This theory stresses on the external factors, so it is a seller-oriented theory. It stresses the importance of the salesperson controlling the situations.

Limitations

This theory does not handle the problem of influencing factors internal to the prospect.

It fails to assign appropriate weight to the response side of the Situation-Response interaction.

"BUYING FORMULA" THEORY OF SELLING

This is a buyer-oriented theory. The late E.K. Strong, Jr. gave the name "buying formula" to this theory. According to this theory, the buyer's needs or problems receive major attention and the salesperson's role is to help the buyer find solutions.

Buying formula is a schematic representation of a group of responses, arranged in psychological sequence. This theory emphasises on the responses of the prospects and does not emphasise on the external factors assuming that being conscious of these factors the salesperson will not overlook them.

Reduced to simplest elements, the mental processes involved in a purchase are as follows:

$$\text{Need (or Problem)} \longrightarrow \text{Solution} \longrightarrow \text{Purchase}$$

Because the outcome of a purchase affects the chance that a continuing relationship will develop between the buyer and the seller, and organisations are interested in continuing relationships it is necessary to add a fourth element. The four elements are:

Need (or Problem) ⟶ Solution ⟶ Purchase ⟶ Satisfaction

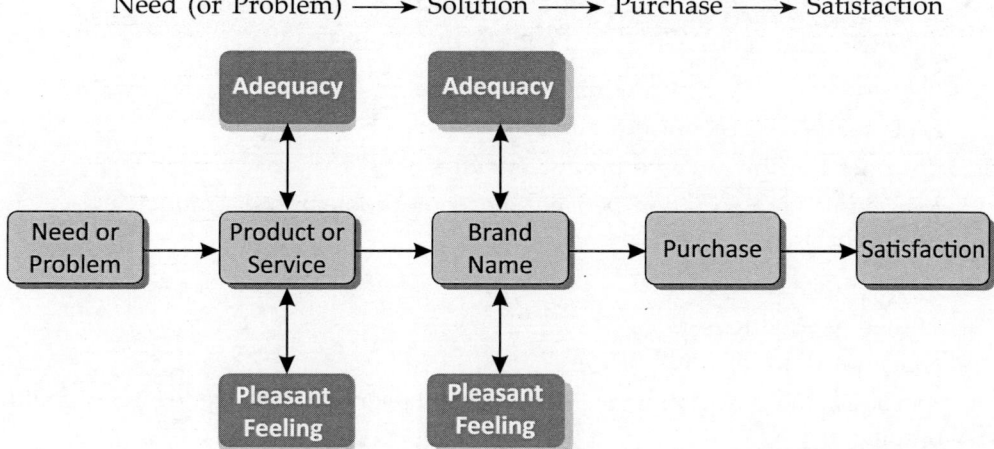

Figure 2.3 Buying Formula Theory
(*Source:* slideshare.net)

In buying, the element "solution" involves 2 parts:

1. Product/Service
2. Trade name (name of manufacturer, company or salesperson)

Upon using the product or service he experiences satisfaction/dissatisfaction.

Need or Problem ⟶ Product/Service

or

Trade Name ⟶ Purchase ⟶ Satisfaction/Dissatisfaction

With adequacy and pleasant feelings included, the buying formula becomes

Adequacy

Need or Problem ⟶ Product Service & Trade Name ⟶ Purchase ⟶ Satisfaction

Pleasant Feelings

When a buying habit is being established, the buyer must know why the product or service is an adequate solution to the need or problem and why the trade name is the best one to buy. The buyers also must have pleasant feeling towards the product or service and the trade name.

The answer to each selling problem is implied in the buying formula and differences among answers are differences in emphasis upon the elements in the formula:

1. If prospect

   Does not feel a need

   Do not recognise a problem

   That can be satisfied by the product/service

   Emphasis: The need or problem should be emphasised

2. If prospect

   Feels the needs/recognise the problem

   But does not think of the product/service

   Emphasis: The association between need or problem and product/service should be emphasised

3. If the prospect:

   Thinks of product/service

   Does not think of trade name

   Emphasis: the association between product/service and trade name should be emphasised.

4. If:

   Need or problem

   Product or service

   Trade name are well associated

   Emphasis: should be upon facilitating purchase and use.

5. If competition is felt:

   Emphasis: establishing in the prospect's minds the adequacy of trade named product/service and pleasant feelings towards it

6. If sales to new prospects are desired

   Emphasis: all the elements

   Need/problem recognition

   Product/service

   Trade name

   Facilitating purchase and use

   Adequacy and pleasant feelings towards trade name

7. If more sales are desired to old customers

   The latter should be reminded

"BEHAVIOURAL EQUATION" THEORY

This theory emphasises the buyer's decision process but also takes the salesperson's influence process into account. JA Howard explains buying behaviour in terms of the purchasing decision process, viewed as phases of the learning process. Four essential elements of the learning process are drive, cue, response and reinforcement:

(i) **Drives:** These are strong internal stimuli that impel the buyer's response. They are of two kinds:

    (a) *Innate drives:* Stem from the physiological needs.

    (b) *Learned drives:* These are acquired and elaborations of the innate drives. For example—striving for status or social approval.

(ii) **Cues:** These are weak stimuli that determine when the buyer will respond.

    (a) *Triggering cues:* activate the decision process for any given purchase.

    (b) Non-triggering cues influence the decision process but do not activate it. It may operate at any time even though the buyer is not contemplating a purchase.

    (c) Specific product and information cues also serve as triggering cues.

(iii) **Response:** This is what the buyer does.

(iv) **Reinforcement:** This is any event that strengthens the buyer's tendency to make a particular response. Howard incorporates these four elements into an equation:

$$B = P \times D \times K \times V$$

Here,

B = Response or the internal response tendency, i.e., act of purchasing a brand

P = Predisposition or the inward response tendency, i.e., force of habit

D = Present drive level or amount of motivation

K = "Incentive potential", i.e., the value of the product or its potential satisfaction to the buyer

V = Intensity of all cues

The relation among the variables is multiplicative. If any independent variable has a zero value, B will also be zero. Example $D = 0$ (individual is motivated), $B = 0$ (No response).

Each time there is a response, a purchase in which satisfaction (K) is sufficient to yield a reward predisposition (P) increases in value

or

When satisfaction yields a reward, reinforcement occurs.

After reinforcement, the probability increases that the buyer will buy the product, the next time the cue appears.

(a) Buyer-Seller Dyad and Reinforcement

Salesperson		Client Relationship
Wishes to sell a product	⟶	Wishes to buy a product
Want feedback	⟶	Wants information about product and its uses
Sales person gives social approval to buyer by displaying high regard with friendly greetings and praise	⟶	Buyer can also provide sellers a good behaviour

(b) Salesperson's Influence Process

$$B = P \times D \times K \times V$$

Salesperson influences all the four elements.

1. Salesperson influences P (predisposition) directly by interacting with the buyers in ways rewarding to the buyer.
2. Salesperson exerts influence through D (amount of motivation).
3. Salesperson can affect K (potential satisfaction of buyer) when buyer has narrowed down the choices to few sellers Salesperson can communicate the merits of the company brand and show how it is relatively better.
4. Salesperson can influence V (the intensity of all cues)—can vary the intensity of his or her effort, so making the difference in V.

(c) Sales Person's Role in Reducing Buyer Dissonance

Reducing pre-and-post decision anxiety or dissonance is an important function of the salesperson. Recognising that the buyer's dissonance varies both according to whether the product is an established or a new one and whether the salesperson-client relationship is ongoing or new; these are four types of cases involving the salesperson's role:

1. An established product—an ongoing salesperson-client relationship:
    ♦ Dissonance would be less.
    ♦ The salesperson is effective because the salesperson is trusted by the buyer.
2. An established product—a new salesperson-client relationship:
    The salesperson, being new, is less effective in reducing dissonance.
3. A new product—an ongoing salesperson-client relationship:
    ♦ The buyer experiences dissonance.
    ♦ Because of the established relationship with the buyer, the salesperson can reduce dissonance.
4. A new product-a new salesperson-client relationship:
    ♦ The buyer needs dissonance reduction.
    ♦ The salesperson is less capable of providing it.

How can a salesperson facilitate the buyer's dissonance reduction?

The two ways are:

1. To emphasise the advantages of the product purchased, while stressing the disadvantages of the forgone alternatives.
2. To show that many characteristics of the chosen item are similar to products the buyer has forgone. But his product is approved by the reference groups. They need reassurance that the decision was a wise one.

MODERN APPROACHES OF SALES

In comparison to earlier times, today the selling of products has become more advanced. Customers nowadays are able to distinguish between genuine products and marketing gimmicks. Customers can easily access information through the Internet and compare the goods or services that are available in the market. It has also become easy to get reviews of products through online forums. Flexible, tailor-made and customised products are being sold by companies nowadays. The organisations make use of various approaches to make buying decisions. Some of the modern approaches are discussed below:

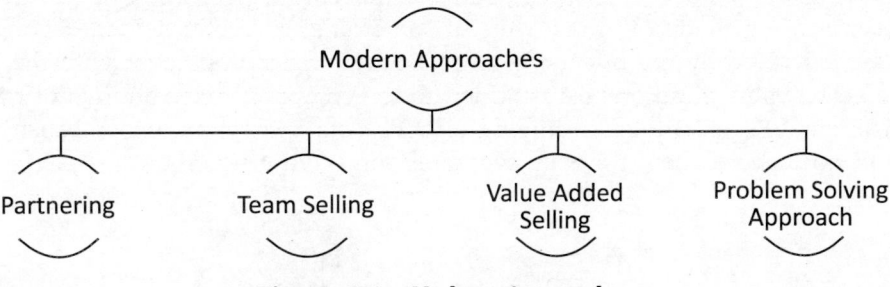

Figure 2.4 Modern Approaches

Partnering

As per this approach, there is a collaboration between the buyer and salesperson and the buyer gets the treatment of a viable partner. The best solution is provided by the buyer through this collaboration. Organisations may even provide lifetime agreements to their partners. They tend to understand the customer's need, beside solving various problems. As sellers prove to be useful resources for the long-term, the customers tend to develop long-term relationships with them. This modern sales approach advocates partnering as it helps in providing two-way benefits.

A salesperson should see through customer's eyes to become a caring and trusted partner. If the salesperson has complete knowledge of the product then only he can link benefits and features. Further, he needs to handle the objections carefully by explaining how the benefits of a product are helpful in making the lives of the customer much better.

Team Selling

When an individual salesperson cannot satisfy the complex buying needs of large buyers then the sellers use team selling. The team is constituted in such a way that they have knowledge of different areas. By working in a co-ordinated and integrated manner, they address the needs of the buyers. Since the members try to achieve higher level of satisfaction so this approach is quite beneficial. The brand can be positioned in a better way by using this approach. It is easier to develop credibility by using a team of sellers. However, this approach should be used when chances for profit and sales are higher as this approach can be expensive for application. Sometimes confusion may be created when different departments have different agendas. Companies need to consider whether they want to use this approach on the basis of the pros and cons. For example, when a team of two technicians and two salespersons gives a presentation for a product then the salespersons explain the uses of the product and technicians explain only the technical part. While working in a team, positive results can be obtained by team members by integrating their mind and work. A synergy effect is brought forth when using this integration of minds.

Value Added Selling

To meet the customer's needs, a salesperson is required. While selling the products, value added services are provided to the buyers. If something extra is provided beyond what is expected or perceived by the buyers. Example, providing laptop cover with the purchase of a laptop. The value addition cost is added to the company's cost and is not transferred to the customers. For example: on buying a toothpaste if they get a toothbrush free then they would not have to spend money separately on buying it.

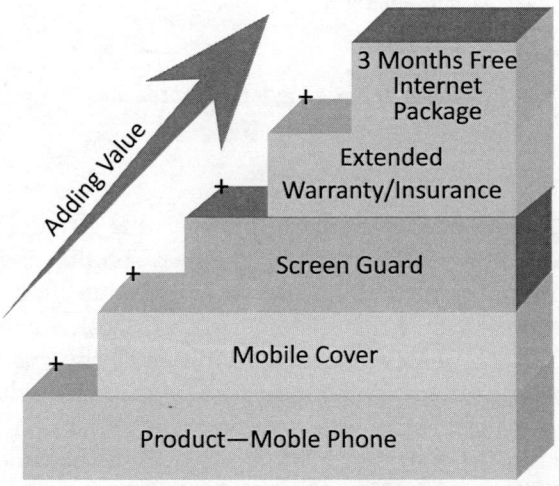

Figure 2.5 Value Addition

Problem Solving Approach/Consultative Selling

The salesperson acts as a problem solver or consultant as per this approach. Matching the needs of the customers to the products or services is his/her job. Every customer seeks a solution to the problem at hand. Only when the salesperson clearly understands the problem, he can solve it. Due to the win-win nature of this approach, it is quite popular. In this approach, the main focus is not the features of the product rather the problems faced by the prospects.

Since the focus of these approaches is to build a long-term relationship with the customer, it is useful to know about the modern sales approaches. When all the information regarding competing products is available to the salesperson, it becomes easier for them to sell the products.

CASE STUDY

Shiv Singh, a sales representative, was doing good business through cold calling. He would enter a building randomly and start chatting with secretaries collecting information like name and designation. He would make around 40 calls per day which included about 5 presentations. He had been salesman for about 12 years and had made about 12000 calls in total. His fast thinking and alertness were the secret to his success.

In contrast, Sohan Singh working for a telemarketing company made unsolicited calls. He would use various techniques of persuading customers so that they may show some interest. If they seemed interested then the call was transferred to another section of the company.

Generally, a set of 15 telemarketers made about 10000 initial contacts and opened at least 20 accounts in a 5-day period. However, the government passed a regulation putting restrictions on unsolicited phone calls. This was done because of complaints made by the customers who did not like to receive telemarketing calls.

Cold calling is often unpopular but sometimes it may prove beneficial when good information is provided. Shiv Singh had main focus on dynamic personal selling. On the other hand, Sohan Singh has more focus on organised technology.

Questions

1. Which of the two companies is going to be impacted by the new rules?
2. Which pattern of cold calling would be preferred by you?

SUMMARY

The chapter deals with the four important theories of selling. There four important theories are: AIDAS theory, right set of circumstances theory, buying-formula theory of selling and behavioural equation theory. Besides these, certain modern approaches to sales are also discussed. In the AIDAS theory the prospect goes through five stages consciously which include Attention, Interest, Desire, Action and Satisfaction. The second theory, "right set of circumstances theory" is also called the "situation-response" theory. The particular circumstances prevailing in a given selling situation cause the prospect to respond in a predictable way. The third theory called buying formula is a schematic representation of a group of responses, arranged in psychological sequence. Lastly, behavioural equation theory emphasises the buyer's decision process but also takes the salesperson's influence process into account. Among the modern approaches: partnering, team selling, value-added selling and consultative selling were discussed. In partnering, there is a collaboration between the buyer and salesperson and the buyer gets the treatment of a viable partner. When an individual salesperson cannot satisfy the complex buying needs of large buyers then the sellers use team selling. In the third approach, while selling the products, value added services are provided to the buyers. The salesperson acts as a problem solver or consultant as per the consultative approach.

KEY TERMS

Money objection: It refers to a situation, where the prospects have limited budget to buy a product.

Price objection: In this situation, the prospect compares the price of the product with its value.

Probing method: This method is used to get further into the detail of information.

Product objection: It refers to the situation, where the prospects have doubts regarding the product performance.

Prospect: The prospect refers to the lead or prospective customer whom the salesperson needs to convince for closing a sales deal.

Selling: Selling is the exchange activity carried by the organisations and individuals to fulfil the needs of the consumers to earn profit in return.

Salesperson: The one who represents the company in front of the customers and is responsible for the sales of goods or services, is known as a salesperson.

EXERCISES

2.1 Briefly explain the Buying Formula theory.

2.2 Explain exhaustively the AIDAS model of selling.

2.3 Discuss exhaustively the right situation hypothesis. Give pertinent guides to make a differentiation among outside and inward factors.

2.4 Team selling has turned into a reasonable device for the organisations to confront the intricacies, in this wake examine the idea of group selling for any modern item.

2.5 What do you mean by consultative selling approach? Examine how a sales rep can turn into an issue solver through models.

2.6 Following customary and present day selling draws near, examine the utility of both the selling strategies exhaustively. Likewise, draw out the distinctions among them referring to applicable models.

3

Process of Personal Selling

LEARNING OBJECTIVES

LO1: To understand the evolution of the selling process

LO2: To identify the steps of the selling process

LO3: To know the methods of prospecting

LO4: To explain pre-approach steps and approach methods

LO5: To understand various methods of sales presentations, demonstration and handling of objections

LO6: To determine techniques used for closing the sale and follow-up

INTRODUCTION

The idea of sales as a science and an art divides sales management into two schools of thought. Some sales managers are of the thought that through proper training salesperson can be groomed for the process of selling. Other successful sales managers believe that selling is an art that some people are better in comparison than others. Both schools of thought agree that a sequence or process is followed which can be planned.

This chapter covers the various steps involved in the selling process. The importance of each step varies depending on the nature and type of service or product, at what stage the product is in the life cycle, the nature of innovation and payment procedures. For example, in well-established industries the majority of objections are related to price whereas in emerging industries like IT, the objections are mainly related to adaptation to technology.

Further, in the case of high-tech products educating the customer and demonstration of the product is important. In business-to-business selling, the seller has to demonstrate the functions of the product whereas in retail selling there is lower significance of the demonstration part. In case of cash-based buying, on the closing of the sales, there is instant transfer of payment but in the case of installment buying, the transfer of ownership takes place long after the real closure of sales.

According to different selling situations, the duty of the salesperson also changes. The primary duty of the salesperson is to provide necessary information to the customers regarding the product and service. This is known as "The knowledge dispensing function" and is important as in its absence it leads to poor buying decisions by the customers. This information is generally available through company websites as well.

EVOLUTION OF PERSONAL SELLING

The nature and structure of personal selling is changing and therefore the following things are no longer tolerated:

- ◆ Selling to the customer by telling anything they want to hear.
- ◆ Being a good talker to convince and influence customers.
- ◆ Immediate closure of the deal.
- ◆ Networking at places like sporting or cultural events would mean done deal.

Personal selling has evolved through following stages:

Price and Traditional features Approach

This approach deals with the customer by explaining the product features in an effort to make the sale. In place of looking for broader organisational objectives, the salesperson generally aimed to make customers happy.

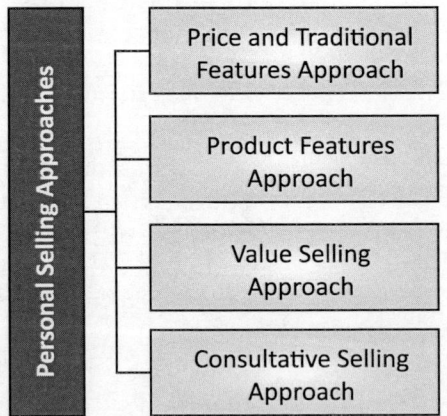

Figure 3.1 Approaches to Personal Selling

Product Features Approach

In this approach the benefits of product or service are explained with a more positive shift. A problem-solving approach is taken which goes beyond just demonstrating the features. This approach works on the notion that to be sustainable and competitive one needs to sell products with value.

Value Selling Approach

This approach seeks to build broader and deeper B2B relationships in place of simple B2C relationships. The company works on a more client-focussed level by seeking qualifiable and quantifiable information.

Consultative Selling Approach

This approach considers the requirement of delivering value to customers after considering the strategic requirements or prospective customers. This comes with application, qualification and identification of strategic value sought by customers.

THE SELLING PROCESS

The same basic steps form part of every selling process, even when the time required to complete it and the detail of each step varies based on the product being sold.

For instance, a door-to-door sales representative may go from prospecting to closing of sales in 15 minutes while moving through all the steps, the selling process for computers may require several visits to get an order.

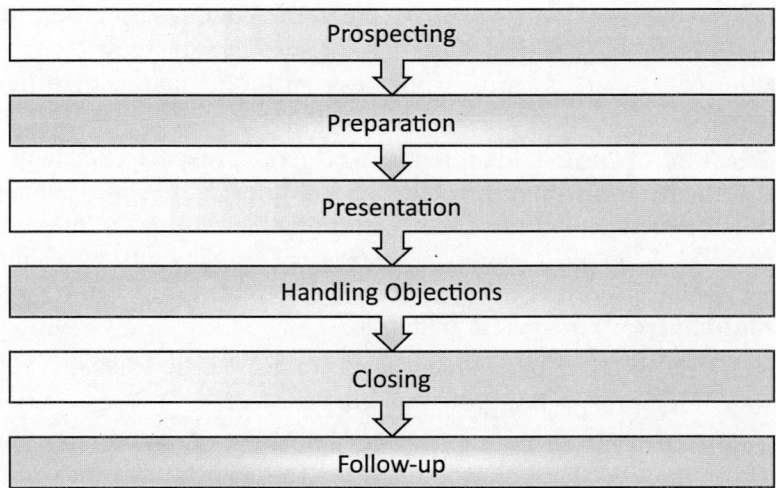

Figure 3.2   Process of Selling

Prospecting

Finding qualified potential customers or prospecting is the first step of the selling process. It is unlikely that customers will come to the salesperson except in retail sales. Potential customers must be sought out in order to sell the product by the salesperson. Certain keywords related to the offering can be searched through the web so that prospects may easily find the product and specially-coded pages are used for this activity which is greatly enhanced today using websites optimised with keywords when they search the web. Once prospecting is underway, poor leads can be screened out and it then is up to the sales professional to identify likely customers by qualifying those prospects further. This qualification process can also be started using *modern websites* which go a long way in identifying potential prospects. There are two major activities involved in prospecting:

1. Prospects, also known as potential customers, are identified.
2. If they are valid prospects then qualify them in order.

(a) Identifying Prospects

♦ It is not an easy job to identify potential customers

♦ Rejection rate is quite high

A few techniques and best sources for finding prospects are:

Present Customers: The existing satisfied customers of a salesperson form the best source of prospects. It is much easier to sell additional goods and services to existing customers than to attract new customers.

Endless Chain: Satisfied customers are the source of referrals. Sales representatives ask current customers to provide names of friends or business associates sales representatives who might be interested in buying similar products or services. The salesperson contacts these prospects, ask for more referrals. Hence, it does not take much time to develop a lengthy list. In many cases, however it is difficult to get a referral cards, so salesperson just takes a letter or a business card. A business card is a small card printed with one's name, occupation, business address, etc.

Centre of Influence: Identification of good prospects can help a salesperson and the person with information about other people or influence over them is called the centre of influence. Such people are found in mainly four spheres: political, religious, business and social. Example: housewives, local politicians etc. Other important influences include celebrities and film personalities who can influence purchasing patterns.

Spotters: In some companies 'sales trainees' called usually Spotters act as a source for prospecting potential customers.

Cold Call: This technique involves knocking on doors in target areas to find  the prospects. The salesperson makes contact with a potential customer, introduces himself and asks if there is a use for the product or service. Generally cold calls result in a later appointment. Therefore, salespersons should select areas with higher prospect density before making the cold calls. This is however a time-consuming process and may not be effective in all cases.

Directories: Directories are full of prospects. Telephone directories and computer databases are potential sources of prospects. A salesperson may also find that for professional societies and trade associations, their

Figure 3.3   Cold Calling   membership directories are good sources for prospects.

Newspapers consisting of information about weddings, business ventures, births and new arrivals in town are also helpful in building sales a pool.

Mailing Lists: In order to attract direct mail advertisers, some companies compile lists of organisations and individuals. These lists may also identify sales prospects. Being more selective and current than directories is the major advantage of mailing lists. However, the response rate is low and follow up procedures like repetition may be implemented to increase the response rate.

Trade Shows and Exhibitions: Advance announcements sent to trade publication helps to attract people. Important prospects can be encouraged to visit company's booth by promising a gift or mailing invitations. The people visiting the trade show register names for demonstration and salespeople can call these people subsequently to make a sale.

Figure 3.4 Trade Show

Telemarketing: There are two types of telemarketing—inbound and outbound. In outbound telemarketing the representatives of the company call the customers, whereas in inbound telemarketing, the prospect calls the company. By providing a toll-free number, the mass media campaign of the companies can be made effective and additional information may be provided. Data collected through inbound telemarketing can be used for making outbound calls.

Online Contact: Using newer technologies, such as video conferencing or text messaging (e.g., online chat) salesperson can contact customers over the internet.

(b) Qualifying Prospects: Once the salesperson has identified potential customers, they must be qualified by him to determine whether they are valid prospects.

Unless validation is done, it is considered waste of time and energy in trying to sell to people who will not or cannot purchase the product or service. There are several factors to consider while qualifying a prospect.

One approach to qualifying is called MAN approach

♦ M—Money

♦ A—Authority

♦ N—Need

Money: Does the prospect have the money or resource to purchase a product or service?

♦ Ability to pay is critical factor in qualifying a prospect.

♦ The salesperson must be familiar with financial resources of a prospect.

Authority: Is commitment making authority available with the prospect?

This is particularly of concern when dealing with corporation, government agencies or other large organisations. In order to economise selling time more effectively, the key decision maker must be identified early on by the salesperson.

Need: Is the product or service needed by the prospect?

♦ A sales call should not be wasted if sales person cannot establish that the customer will benefit from purchasing a product/service.

♦ Either the prospect will end up dissatisfied with the purchase or will refuse the offer.

The salesperson should before proceeding further, first appraise whether need, authority and money exist with the prospect.

Preparation

After the qualification of the prospect upon identification, the salesperson prepares for the sale of service or product. Two key activities are involved in the preparation stage as follows:

(a) **Pre-approach:** The prospect, his needs and situation can be better understood by the pre-approach step as it includes all the information gathering activities necessary to learn relevant facts.

Four steps necessary for pre-approach are:

(i) It should qualify the lead or disclose the party need and ability to buy.

(ii) For tailoring the presentation according to the prospect, the necessary information should be provided by the seller.

(iii) During the presentation to avoid making serious errors by providing information that may keep the sales person updated.

(iv) Finally, a good pre-approach increases the sales persons confidence enabling him to handle whatever may arise during the sales.

(b) **Call planning:** A specific planning sequence is involved with call planning.

   (i) The objective of call is defined by the salesperson, then a selling strategy is devised to achieve this objective and the appointment is made.

   (ii) Getting an order is the primary objective of any sales effort.

   (iii) Intermediate objectives may be needed for some sales call as:

      ♦ To get more information about the prospect.

      ♦ To relate the prospects concerns and needs to benefits and features of the service or product.

      ♦ Demonstrating the product after obtaining permission.

      ♦ To introduce a new distribution.

      ♦ To settle past collection disputes/collections.

   (iv) Formulating "A Tailor-Made Strategy" after carefully considering the prospect's needs and background is required in order to be able to appropriately lure the prospect.

   (v) Since sales calls are costly, they should be arranged in advance.

Presentation

Giving the formal sales presentation. How the product meets the special needs of the customers is the main objective of the presentation.

The salesperson informed the prospect about:

(a) The availability, capabilities and characteristics of goods and services that are for sale.

(b) Presentation should be interesting enough to keep the attention of the prospect focussed on the proposal. Communication skills of the presenter are very important.

(c) Sales presentation is classified into five different categories:

   (i) **Fully-automated:** It is the most highly structured approach, based on audio-visual, film, or slide presentation. The sales person simply answers questions, or clears up doubts. For example: selling life insurance to the rural prospects.

   (ii) **Semi-automated:** When necessary, the sales person adds comments to the prepared materials read from literatures and brochures.

   (iii) **Memorised:** A Company prepared message is presented with a few changes by the sales person. Visual aids may or may not be used in this case.

   (iv) **Organised:** Organised presentation is often the most effective and the most popular sales presentation method. Salesperson has complete flexibility in verbal communication, but follows a company prepared outline or checklist. The customers are moved through four stages to a purchase decision, i.e. "attention, interest, desire and action" (AIDA) in the selling process.

(v) **Unstructured:** The real sources of the company's needs include the seller and buyer who together explore the problems. They are often effective and widely used but they have a number of limitations like time is wasted, points are often missed and they are not too well-focused. The use of unstructured method is difficult to be taught to sales persons.

Another form of categorisation includes canned, organised and tailored presentations. Each is different based on the modifications made by the salesperson.

Canned Presentation: It is prepared by the company and designed by experienced people in the organisation. New salespersons can use it to address the queries of the customers. This type of presentation helps in confidence building but it is very mechanical and non-enthusiastic in nature.

Organised Presentation: This type of presentation is based on company policy and systems but there is enough scope for wording the presentation. This type of presentation is flexible and helpful for both new and experienced salespersons. The presentation is developed on the basis of information collected from field research.

Tailored Presentation: It is designed specifically for a particular customer by performing a detailed evaluation of the business of prospective customer. For business-to-business selling, this is the most commonly used method. This method is more suitable for experienced salespersons as it is quite time-consuming.

Approach and demonstration include the two distinct activities of sales presentation.

Approach

In the actual approach, the sales person has the name of the prospect and adequate pre-approach information. The entire presentation is frequently broken or made by this step. A good approach does three things:

♦ It gets the attention of the prospect.

♦ Hearing more about the proposition immediately inspires interest.

♦ Gets easily transitioned into the demonstration phase can be made.

Four commonly used basic approaches are:

1. **The Introductory Approach:** The salesperson introduces himself to the prospect and states which company he represents to.

2. **The Product Approach:** It consists of handling the product to prospect with little conversation. It can be most effective when the product is unique and creates interest on sight.

3. **The Customer Benefit Approach:** By informing the prospect of what the firm can provide in benefits.

4. **Referral Approach:** For meeting a new prospect, the permission of a present or past customer is sought to use his name as a reference.

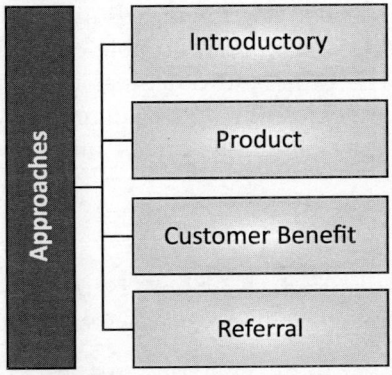

Figure 3.5   Approaches

Asking right questions at right time is known as probing. During the selling process, probing takes place in different stages. In order to learn more about the customer demands and gain additional insights, the salesperson performs the action of probing. Mainly primary data is gathered using closed-ended and open-ended questions. The second part of probing involves listening carefully to the answers of the customers. It includes listening to what the customer says and also that he does not say but mean to say.

Demonstration

Core of the selling process is the demonstration. To make a customer, the sales person actually attempts to persuade the prospect and transmits the information through product demonstration. To prepare an effective product demonstration the following two factors should be taken into consideration:

(i) The possibility of even a minor malfunction can be reduced by carefully rehearsing the demonstration.

(ii) Wherever possible "hands on" experience with the product should be designed for the customers as part of the demonstration.

Handling Objections

All salesperson confronts sales resistance, i.e. statements or actions by a prospects that postpone, hinder or prevent the competition of the sales. An objection which can be hidden or stated takes form of sales resistance.

Stated: A chance is given to the sales person to answer to the prospects and they may state their objections to a proposition openly. Reading the prospect's mind is not needed by the salesperson as this is an ideal situation because everything is out in the open.

Hidden: Normally prospects real reasons for not buying are hidden by the prospects. So, marketer must discover hidden objections for which two suggested techniques are:

1. By asking probing questions the salesperson should be in regular communication with the prospect.

2. Use insights gained through experience, combined with a knowledge of the prospects situation to perceive the hidden objection.

All the objections should be met effectively to suit to the customer's demand.

Price objections of prospects due to unaffordable or too high price can be handled by persuading the prospects on the value and outcomes instead of price.

If the salesperson has an extensive knowledge of both their own product and competitor's product, the product objections can be answered best.

Closing

After having overcome and answered objections, asking for the order from the prospects is done in this stage by sales person. There are several techniques for closing:

- **Superior Feature Method:** In this method the salesperson accepts the objections and in turn persuades customers by providing additional benefits of the product. Thus, the customer may agree to buy the product.

- **In Action Close Technique:** The sales person takes an action that will complete the sale. In case of high-priced products, the sales person may negotiate with the financial institution for financial assistance for the prospects.

- **Gift Close Technique:** It provides the prospect with an added incentive for taking immediate buying action.

- **One More Yes Close Technique:** The salesperson restates the benefits of the products in a series of questions that will result in positive responses by the prospects. He slowly removes objection from the customer's mind by tactful handling of arguments. The process may result in an order.

- **Reverse English Method:** In this technique, the salesperson works only on the objections raised by the customers. He works on changing the objections into the basis of buying.

- **Direct Close Technique:** It is a clear and simple technique. The sales person summarises the major points, and asks for the sale. When the buying motives are strong positive then it is the best approach.

- **Pass Out Method:** In this method, the salesperson keeps a neutral opinion. He does not pay attention to the objections especially when they are baseless. The customer may feel neglected but it is suggested to pass off such objections without attending to them.

Experienced sales person always tries to close early. If they are not successful, they continue the presentation and then try a different closing technique. Closing is the most important aspect of the sales process. Unless the sales person can close the sales effectively, the other steps in the sales process are meaningless.

Follow-up

Merely making the sale does not complete the selling process. An important part of the selling process is the after sales activities. Improvement in the chance that the person will buy again in the future are possible with effective sales follow-up which reduces the buyer's doubt about the product or services. The salesperson is also required to maintain good customer relationships. Personal visits, letters, phone calls, greetings, gifts are good ways to keep in touch with customers.

It also is a good way to enhance the goodwill of the company. Corrective actions can be taken during this part of the process. The salesperson may also conduct a self-analysis by making a call to identify his/her strengths and weaknesses in disseminating the knowledge about the product or service. Lastly, it helps to assure that the order will not get cancelled. Further, it paves the way for establishing future relationship with customers and building confidence.

CASE STUDY

When Jai Verma, Chief Executive Officer of OM Consultants received a mail from 3M Hydraulics, he immediately talked over the intercom to his vice-president, Chirag Madan. "If you succeed to get this order and execute the same to the complete satisfaction of 3M Hydraulics, it would open doors for many more orders in future," said the CEO.

"Yes, I agree with you, but for that I will have to fly to Ahmedabad immediately to meet the key people in 2M Hydraulics and to understand clearly their needs, before submitting our proposal," responded Chirag Madan.

"Why not, go ahead, and let me know if you need any help from me," said Jai and hung up. On checking the website of the 3M Hydraulics company, Chirag found that the company had tie-up with a French Company and wanted to manufacture and market hydraulic accessories, pumps and valves. The company had decided on a distribution strategy of selling its products with the help of dealers who were expected to service hydraulic packs, along with their selling, assembling and designing for various applications for materials movements. Chirag spoke with Chaitanya, General Manager of 3M Hydraulics and fixed an appointment for meeting.

Chirag gathered information about market potential for Hydraulic Components in major metros and cities, requirements and competition of 3M Hydraulics. His doubt about "Can we get dealers in India performing so many tasks", was answered by the French manager, "If we can get them in France, why not in India?"

Chirag came back to his office at Pune, discussed with Jai and sent his proposal to Chaitanya. Within 5 days, Chirag received a call from Chaitanya asking him to come over to Ahmedabad for the presentation to a team of top executives, to be followed by negotiation.

Questions
1. How was OM Consultants approach to the requirements of the customer?
2. If you were Chirag Madan, which presentation method, negotiation style and closing technique would be used by you?

SUMMARY

This chapter explains the process of personal selling. The selling process is defined as process through which salespersons can locate and identify prospects, approach them, make presentations, handle objections and close the sale. The process has to be adapted according to the industry in which it is being used. The process usually consists of several steps. The selling activities of salespeople are focussed around the various steps of selling process. These are—prospecting and qualifying, pre-approach, approach, presentation and demonstration, overcoming objections, trial close and follow-up. The chapter explains various techniques for prospecting, presentations, handling customer objections, and closing the sale. The salespersons need to be trained according to these activities so that there exists an effective selling process.

KEY TERMS

Approach: It is one of the steps of the selling process in which the salesperson meets with the buyer for the first time.

Closing: It is one of the steps of the selling process, in which the salesperson helps the buyer to make a buying decision. It is also called closing or concluding the sale, or getting the purchase order from the customer.

Pre-approach: This is one of the steps in the selling process in which the salesperson collects information about the prospect and plans the sales call on the prospect. It is also called precall planning.

Prospecting: It is an activity of finding or searching people or organisations who need and have an ability to buy the product or service offered by the company.

Qualifying: The probable prospect, or sales lead is qualified as a prospect or potential customer if the person or the firm has a need for the product or service, the authority to make the buying decision, and the financial resources to pay.

Trial close: It is one of the steps in the sales process in which the salesperson checks the attitude or the opinion of the prospect to the sales presentation by asking certain questions. If the response is favourable, the salesperson closes the sale.

EXERCISES

3.1 What is the difference between a prospect, suspect, and sales lead? How the probable prospects are qualified?

3.2 In what manner the approach step is different than the pre-approach step? Describe briefly different approach techniques used by salespeople.

3.3 How salespeople understand prospect's needs?

3.4 Explain the difference between a trial close and a close.

3.5 Discuss why a salesperson's job is not over even after getting an order.

4

Strategic Salesforce Planning, Sales Forecasting and Budgeting

LEARNING OBJECTIVES

LO1: To know salesforce planning and strategic planning

LO2: To understand the development of sales strategies to ensure sales growth

LO3: To explain the types of sales forecasts, forecasting approaches, methods and selection of forecasting methods

LO4: To organise the sales budget and know its purpose as well as the budgeting process

INTRODUCTION

The importance of strategic planning is due to its role in sales and marketing functions.

Strategic planning is a process in which an organisation's leaders define their vision for the future and identify their organisation's goals and objectives.

Sales planning is a set of strategies that are designed to help sales teams reach their target sales quotas and help the company reach its overall sales goals.

FEATURES OF SALESFORCE PLANNING

◆ Identifying and arranging priorities before setting the plan.

◆ Next the allocation of resources is done. It is ensured by the manager that until the desired goals are achieved the time and resources are efficiently used.

◆ Developing strong working teams is the next important feature of the salesforce planning. This is done so as to strengthen internal and external partnerships. This helps in easy sharing of information and resources. Further, it helps in improving advertising and new business products.

- ♦ Another important feature is to check the predictability of the process by planning the budgeting process in advance.
- ♦ Finally, a team of people with required experience and involvement in similar processes is created.

BENEFITS OF SALESFORCE PLANNING

- ♦ **User Friendly:** Team members can easily implement it in business.
- ♦ **Quicker Implementation:** The implementation is frequent and if there is experienced salesforce then the process becomes quick.
- ♦ **Built in Reporting:** When implementing salesforce planning, it includes side by side documenting of situations that led to a particular decision which works as a built-in reporting system.

STRATEGIC PLANNING

Strategic planning includes action plan, strategies, long-term objectives and company's mission. There are three organisational levels:

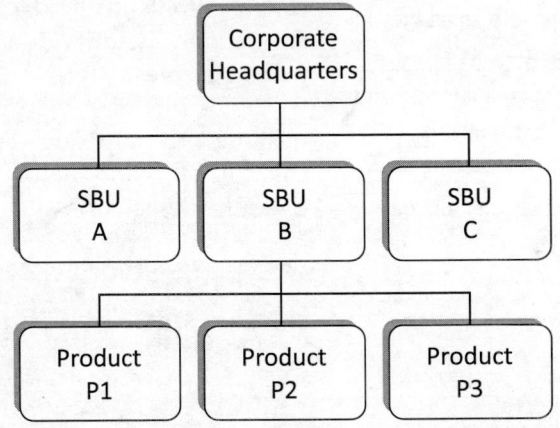

Figure 4.1   Planning at Different Organisational Levels

1. **Corporate Strategic Plan:** To guide the whole organisation corporate strategic planning is developed by the organisations. The planning process includes following activities:
   - (i) Development of corporate mission and objectives.
   - (ii) Defining of strategic business units.
   - (iii) Allocation of resources to strategic business units.
   - (iv) Development of corporate strategies for filling strategic planning gap.

2. **Division and Business Units' Strategic Plans (SBU):** The head of the business unit is given the task of business units' strategic planning. The strategic planning process includes following steps:

   (i) Defining the mission of business unit.

   (ii) Scanning the external environment.

   (iii) Analysing the internal environment.

   (iv) Developing the long-term goals and objectives.

   (v) Formulation of strategies for achievement of goals and objectives.

   (vi) Preparing programs or action plans from the strategies.

   (vii) Implementing the strategies and action-plans.

   (viii) Monitoring results and taking corrective actions.

3. **Product or Functional Plans:** Within a business unit the functional planning for each product is done. Usually plans for short periods of time are developed by functional managers. They focus on routine tasks such as dispatching goods, recruiting people, material purchase, production and sales.

ROLE OF MARKETING AND SALES

These are developed at three organisational levels:

1. **Corporate:** The role of marketing at corporate level is to provide information on competition and customer and advocacy of customer orientation. Analytic driven business decisions are being adopted by many organisations. It means there are large chunks of data, hidden insights and patterns.

2. **Business Unit:** The role of marketing at business unit is to (i) analyse competitive advantage, (ii) developing positioning, targeting and segmenting, and (iii) understanding and forecasting external environment and carry out an analysis of customers and competitors.

3. **Functional:** The role of marketing at functional level is to (i) allocate resources, (ii) coordinate marketing related activities, and (iii) develop marketing mix strategies and implementing them.

STRATEGIC ISSUES

1. **Strategic Thinking Process:** Unknown areas are unexpectedly met when a senior executive is faced with a situation needing strategic decision making. By asking strategic questions these unknown or uncertain areas can mostly be recorded accurately.

2. **Social Selling:** Social selling includes the use of social media for interacting directly with prospective customers, offering product or service fulfilling needs of buyers, answering queries of customers and dealing directly with prospective customers.

SALES STRATEGY

Four parts of an effective sales strategy are as follows:

Figure 4.2 Framework for Sales Strategy

1. **Customer Classification Strategy:** Individual customers are classified into different customer groups within a target market segment. For example, customers are classified into three customer segments:
   - Class A—High profit and sales potential customers.
   - Class B—Medium profit and sales potential customers.
   - Class C—Low profit and sales potential customers.

2. **Customer Relationship Strategy:** Buyers and sellers particularly in business markets have some kind of business relationships. Following are the characteristics of different customer relationship strategies:
   - *Transactional Relationship:* In a transactional relationship, less loyalty is shown to suppliers by the customers. People of Class C belong to this category.
   - *Value-added Relationship:* This includes customers who belong to Class B. Here the focus is on meeting needs better than competitors, offering better solutions, understanding needs of customers and the future and present problems.
   - *Collaborative Relationship:* These are customers belonging to the class A. Trust and commitment are the foundations of a collaborative relationship. In order to earn and retain their business, a mutually satisfying and long-term relationship is aimed at by the buyers and sellers.

3. **Selling Methods:** The various methods of selling include consultative selling, team selling, need-satisfaction method, formula method and stimulus response method.

4. **Marketing Channel Strategy:** Selecting appropriate marketing channel is another issue in the sales strategy. For making a product or service available to customers, the various marketing channels available are: (i) brokers and commission merchants, (ii) internet, (iii) telemarketing by using telephone, (iv) manufacturer's representatives, (v) industrial distributors, and (vi) personal selling through company salespeople.

SALES FORECASTING

The prediction of sales as the sales are expected in a specific future period of time is known as sales forecast. It is an integral part of marketing information system.

Concept

Sales forecast comprised how much of the product is likely to be sold at a specific time period in future in specific markets at specific prices.

Sales Potential

It is the estimate of the maximum possible sales opportunities for a specific company for a particular time period.

Planning Style

There are primarily two planning styles—bottom up and top down. In bottom-up planning, different departments prepare their plans and objectives and present them to the top management. This style is in line with the theory Y of management that people like to work and are committed to the plans formulated by them. On the contrary, the top-down style is related to theory X of management which suggests that people dislike work and usually like to be directed about when and how to do a task.

The preparation of the budget begins at the lowest levels in a sales organisation. This lowest level in the budgetary procedure is the profit center. This budget includes all other expenses and light, heat and rent. Further, it includes the salaries of the sales personnel as well as various expenses incurred.

The various levels of management approve the budget for which they are responsible. In every instance, a description for the coming period is submitted for justification and support. This information helps evaluation of the budget that is submitted. The changes made in the budget in turn impact the plans made.

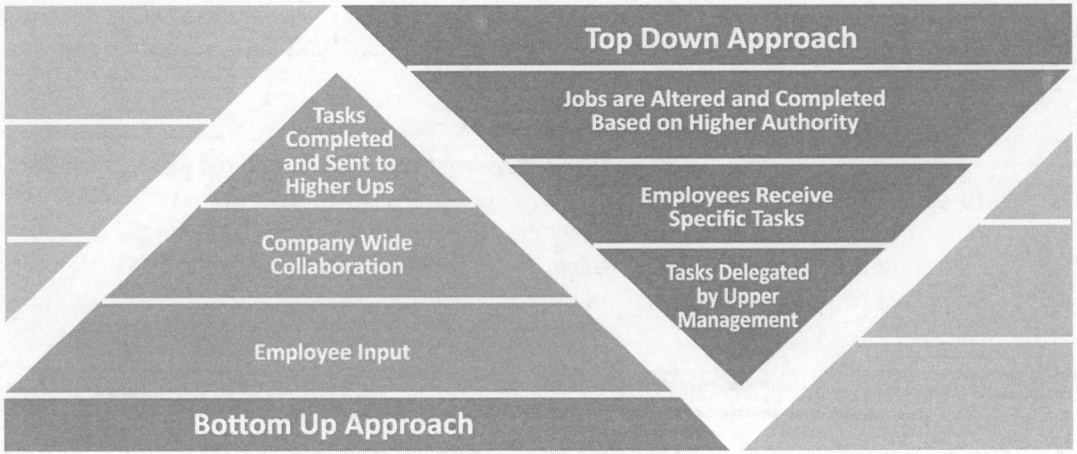

Figure 4.3 Planning Styles

PROCESS OF SALES FORECASTING

The process involves:

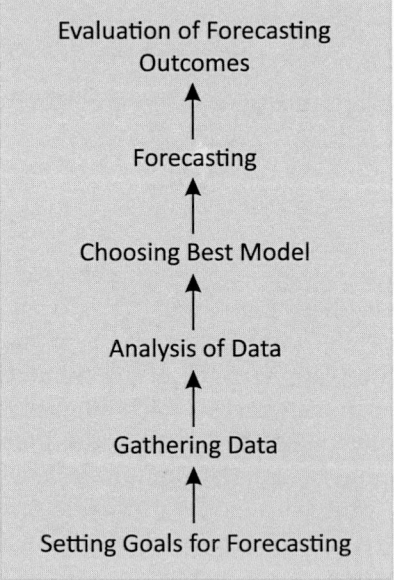

Figure 4.4 Sales Forecasting Process

1. **Determination of Goals:** The sales forecasting goals must be determined by the sales manager. The goals include estimation of income and expenditure, working capital requirements and sales quota.

2. **Collection of Data:** Collecting data regarding the future demand of a product. Analysing the market's potential requires finding out who buys the product and who uses it.

3. **Analysis of Data:** Analysis is a two-step process which includes—selecting factors associated with demand of a product and eliminating segments which do not contain prospective buyers.

4. **Choosing Best Model:** Based on the sales objectives, a suitable method of forecasting must be chosen. For this it is required that information is collected from reliable sources.

5. **Forecasting:** Based on the analysis, future projections must be made. Forecasting may be done either for individual market segments or the entire market.

6. **Evaluation of Outcomes:** There are elements of uncertainty in every forecast. So, the outcomes must be evaluated to assess whether an accurate forecast has been made or it needs amendments.

METHODS FOR FORECASTING SALES

Qualitative Methods

1. Jury Method/Executive Opinion Method

Using this method, a company invites opinions of consultants and executives having knowledge of trends in sales. On the basis of opinions, future sales were forecasted. On the basis of past performance this estimate is made.

2. Survey of Expert Opinion

Based on the opinion of buyers and consumers, the survey is made. It is not useful for consumer goods but only for industrial products. According to this method, first of all potential consumers/buyers are selected by company.

3. Delphi Method

It is a type of expert opinion, which is used to make future estimates related to sales forecasting. A sequence of questionnaires is used to interrogate the experts belonging to a field. The available information is passed down to all members from the limited members who have the required information. The reactions and opinions are analysed—interchanges are permitted and final forecast is presented.

4. Sales Force Composite Method

Salesforce makes the sales forecast. All salesmen develop forecasts in their territory. The aggregate and regional level consolidated at branch are called territory-wise forecasts.

5. User Expectation Method

For industrial products this method is well suited. Various sales are forecasted based on the demand of the product. The users of various products are determined.

Methods of Forecasting Sales	1.	Jury Method/Executive Opinion Method
	2.	Survey of Expert Opinion
	3.	Delphi Method
	4.	Sales Force Composite Method
	5.	User Expectation Method
	6.	Market Share Method
	7.	Analytical Methods
	8.	Market Survey Methods
	9.	Simulation and Econometric Model Building

Figure 4.5 Various Methods of Sales Forecasting

6. Market Share Method

This method makes use of brand preference, company's competitive position and past trend to analyse market share.

Quantitative Methods

7. Analytical Methods

There are several types of analytical methods which include:

Simple Projection Method: It follows the formula as given below:

$$\text{Next year sale} = \frac{(\text{This Year Sales})^2}{\text{Last Year Sales}}$$

Moving Average Method: The irregular effects of trends in sales are eliminated by this method. In this method the weighted average of number of sales is taken.

Time Series Analysis: For long-term forecasts this method is most suited and it is similar to projection method. Analysis is made on the basis of sales fluctuations that are underlying:

1. Long-term growth trend.
2. Seasonal variations.
3. Cyclical changes.
4. Random or irregular fluctuations.

Regression Analysis: In this method dependent values are forecasted by establishing a relationship between variables using a cased forecasting model. The main steps of using regression analysis for sales forecasting include:

♦ Identification of variables dealing with sales of the company.

♦ Determination of the values of variables identified in first step.

♦ Derivation of sales forecast from the above-mentioned estimation.

8. Market Survey Methods

Generally, surveys are taken by companies to learn about satisfaction, preference, beliefs and people's knowledge so that their magnitude in general population can be measured.

9. Simulation and Econometric Model Building

It is an attractive method of sales forecasting for companies marketing durable goods. This method uses a system of equations for representing relationships among different independent variables and sales. Then after values of variables are put in, sales forecast can be made. The sales equation can be written in the following manner:

$$TS = R + N$$

Where,

TS = Total sales

R = replacement demand (purchases made to replace product units going out of use)

N = new-owner demand (purchases to add to the toltal stock of the product in users' possession)

SALES FORECASTS FOR NEW PRODUCTS

These are based on:

1. **Past Records and Experiences:** For making an estimate of sales forecast for new products it is best to keep a record of experiences of previous employees or earlier estimates.

2. **Study of Competing Demand of Products:** It is important that a study is made of competing demand for various products.

3. **Findings of Market Research:** Market research is useful in making forecasting decisions. The data collected through market research helps in making good decisions.

4. **Results of Test Marketing:** Test marketing is also useful in collecting data regarding opinion for new products.

5. **Rate of Substitution:** Information should also be collected regarding substitutes for a product.

IMPROVING SALES FORECAST

The forecasts must be examined by:

1. **Probing into Forecast Methodology:** The forecast methodology must be explained in detail so the sales forecast can be managed easily.

2. **Probing Expert Wisdom to Arrive at an Agreeable Forecasting Level:** Expert advice must be taken so that a consensus can be reached easily regarding the method of forecasting to be used.

3. **Looking at the Terms and Definitions:** When collecting the data, the terms and definitions related to forecasting must be made clear so that there is no confusion.

4. **Constructing Retrospective-prospective Analysis:** By using executive judgement and fine-tuning historical data, an estimate regarding sales forecast can be made.

SALES BUDGETING

A Sales budget is "a financial plan depicting how resources should best be allocated to achieve the forecasted sales". The main purpose of sales budgeting is to achieve the desired sales objectives through planning and controlling the expenditure on resources like people, material, money and facilities.

Purpose of Sales Budget

Three basic purposes of sales budget are:

Planning: The sales manager prepares plan by outlining essential costs to be incurred. This helps in achieving sales objectives and goals.

Coordination: The budget act as an instrument of coordination. Selling is one of the functions of marketing and budget helps in integrating it with other functions like sales, finance, production, purchase, etc.

Control: The sales manager can plan better and spot problem areas. The factors causing variations in result based on comparison of budgeted and actual costs are identified.

Significance of a Sales Budget

The importance of sales budget can be understood from the factors mentioned below:

- ♦ The performance of the sales personnel, regions, products, marketing channels and customers can help in measuring the progress/performance of the organisation.
- ♦ The areas in which the company wants to strengthen or improve its performance are identified by the company.
- ♦ For keeping constant watch on profit of the company and controlling the expenses related with the sales activity.

METHODS OF SALES BUDGETING

Zero Base Budgeting: This process involves initiation from zero base for creating sales budget for every year. It justifies all expenditures while discarding conventions. The only disadvantage of this method is that it is time consuming and prolonged.

Task and Objective Method: In this method budgets are developed by marketers through identification of sales function. Then the related tasks are ascertained through selling for achieving objectives.

Percentage of Sales: Many companies set a specified percentage of sales as their sales budget.

Executive Judgement: For each expense category, the judgement of sales manager is used for deciding budgeted selling expenses. The senior sales executives provide opinions based on sales and marketing plans.

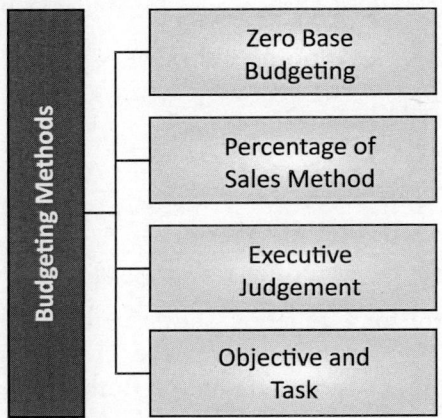

Figure 4.6 Budgeting Methods

SALES BUDGET PROCESS

Review the Situation: A review should be made of the future, current as well as the past budget performance. The review helps to understand the deviations of actual performance from the budget. The review of future sales helps to assess the changing environment.

Communication: The format, timetable, assumptions and guidelines must be communicated to the field sales managers by the head of sales function. The estimates regarding service to be sold, average selling price and sales volume in units are to be made by the first level field sales manager.

Preparation of Subordinate Budgets: It is the budget prepared by both the middle level managers as well as the first level sales managers. The middle level mangers use technique such as moving average, whereas first level mangers use build up or bottom-up approach.

Approval of Sales Budget: The national level manager in consultation with marketing manager makes the alternative proposals of sales budget to be presented before the top managers. The sales budget gets approved after detailed discussion with the top management.

Other Departments: After approval the budget is finally given to the various departments like human resource, materials, finance and production. Therefore, the budget is broken down into monthly and quarterly periods for each sales territory.

Implementation

For every item of the budget a standard is set for which performance is measured. In case of variance the following actions are available:

1. For ascertaining whether poor performance is due to variance. If this is true then budget expenses need to be brought into line for which necessary steps must be taken.

2. The budget must be revised according to changing conditions. For example, if there is an increase in travel expenses because a customer was not covered previously then action should be taken for revising the budget.

The variation mainly arises because of the following:

♦ Fringe benefits and salaries.

♦ Direct expenses of selling.

♦ Company vehicle maintenance.

♦ Business promotion costs and sales.

♦ Allowances of promotion including rebates and discounts.

Normally, the procedure for budgeting starts in the sales department as it is major department for generation of revenue flow. Once the tentative approval for the sales budget is received, the budget outlines can be prepared by other departments.

CASE STUDY

Environmental threats and opportunities must be responded for effective sales management. Environmental influences comprise of legal, political, economic, technological, cultural and social. Core i5 processor is in much demand in market due to its processing speed which gives a quick access to information. The sales people have more access to current and accurate data which is useful in selling.

Incentives motivate sales manager but the health of the economy has repercussions. In times of difficulty the company tries to reduce sales incentives as they are unable to keep up with the expenses. Opposite approach is taken by some companies as they increase incentive programs and morale of salespeople. According to the health of the economy, there is variation in types of incentives.

Sales managers must monitor changes in legal environment. The way in which managers manage and sales people sell is affected by it. For business people the most important skill required is the ability to adapt to changes. The success of the company is determined by it.

Questions

1. Discuss whether during tough times, the incentives must be lowered or increased.

2. With the demand of Core i5 and other high technology equipment the time spent by salesman with customers gets reduced. Is this a problem or not?

SUMMARY

Developing strong working teams is an important feature of the salesforce planning. This is done so as to strengthen internal and external partnerships. This helps in easy sharing of information and resources. Further, it helps in improving advertising and new business products. It is required that sales managers can assess outcomes and based on current decisions they can provide future implications. The strategic planning is mostly done by top managers whereas the short-term goals are planned by middle level managers. The prediction of sales as the sales are expected in a specific future period of time is known as sales forecast. It is an integral part of marketing information system. A Sales budget is "a financial plan depicting how resources should best be allocated to achieve the forecasted sales". The main purpose of sales budgeting is to achieve the desired sales objectives through planning and controlling the expenditure on resources like people, material, money and facilities.

KEY TERMS

Sales budgeting: A sales budget is management's estimation of sales for a future financial period. A company uses sales budgets in order to set department goals, estimate earnings and forecast production requirements.

Sales forecasting: Sales forecasting is the process of estimating future revenue by predicting the amount of product or services a sales unit (which can be an individual salesperson, a sales team, or a company) will sell in the next week, month, quarter, or year.

Sales planning: Sales planning is a set of strategies that are designed to help sales teams reach their target sales quotas and help the company reach its overall sales goals.

EXERCISES

4.1 Discuss the features and benefits of salesforce planning.

4.2 Explain in detail about strategic planning and strategic issues.

4.3 What is sales forecasting? Explain its importance.

4.4 Describe the various methods of sales forecasting.

4.5 What is the purpose and significance of sales budgeting?

4.6 Describe the methods of sales budgeting.

4.7 How is salesforce budgeting implemented?

5

Sales Organisation

INTRODUCTION

After an organisation decides its strategies and goals, the implementation of strategies and action plans takes place with the help of sales organisation.

A sales organisation "is an organisation of individuals either working together for the marketing of products and services manufactured by an enterprise or for products that are procured by the firm for the purpose of reselling."

This chapter discusses the purpose of sales organisation, types of sales organisation and its size.

PURPOSE OF SALES ORGANISATION

In order to carry out the various tasks effectively and efficiently, the sales organisation structure must be evolved in such a way that it assists the sales managers. Therefore, the purpose of a sales organisation is to:

♦ **Ensuring a Reasonable Span of Control:** The number of individuals reporting to a sales manager is known as span of control. Generally, a span of control should be around 6–8. However, according to recent trends there is reduction in hierarchy levels leading to flatter structures. Based on the abilities and job description of the subordinates, the span of control is decided.

♦ **Achieving Effective Coordination:** In order to achieve the firms' objectives, all functions should interact harmoniously. However, harmony does not exist between departments due to distrust and rivalries. In a typical organisation, employees need to work together to satisfy customers for which effective coordination is required.

♦ **Showing Market Orientation:** By having a market-oriented organisation structure, an adequate response can be provided by the companies. There are several segments for consumers and business belonging to the present and potential customers. The segment served by the marketing team is developed using the appropriate sales strategy.

♦ **Defining Line and Staff Positions:** People in a line position have authority and responsibility for achieving the major goals of the organisation. Line managers are responsible for achieving sales targets and performing sales management activities. On the other hand, the advisory and suggestive authority is given to staff managers.

♦ **Allowing Degree of Specialisation:** Generally, sales management tasks are performed by sales managers whereas selling activities are performed by salespersons. The specialist approach becomes more effective as the complexity of the market grows and the number of salespersons increases.

♦ **Determining the Degree of Centralisation:** Authority and responsibility are placed at higher levels of management in a centralised structure. These responsibilities are delegated in a decentralised organisation. However, no company is completely centralised or decentralised as some activities are centralised to minimise costs and others are decentralised for better control.

ROLE OF SALES ADMINISTRATION

In an ideal sales department, cooperation would be maximised, friction would be minimised, duplication of effort would we eliminated and wastage of motion is reduced. On providing sufficient attention to the sales organisation, ideal can be approached and productive sales efforts can be made.

♦ **Specialists Developed:** With the expansion of business, sales and marketing activities become complex. When executives are reluctant to delegate authority, it is difficult to fix the responsibility of all activities related to performance. One purpose of organising sales activities is to facilitate delegation of authority. The chief means of achieving reorganisation is division of labour or specialisation.

♦ **Assurance for the Performance of Necessary Activities:** With the growth of sales organisation, it becomes important to perform all necessary activities. The meaning of "necessary" changes with time. In case of specialised jobs, it is mandatory that each job is assigned to specific individual. However, if tasks are not assigned to specific individuals they may not be performed. Small companies have direct contact with customers, whereas when companies become large, they lose contact with customers. In such situations it required that someone is given the task of maintaining this relationship.

◆ **Achievement of Balance:** A perfect organisation achieves balance or coordination. Individuals differ in terms of effectiveness, potential and competence. A sound organisation may not function smoothly if the executives are particularly forceful. They may have personalities which may cause failure to delegate due to which their importance is mismatched with their position. An organisation can achieve more when members work collectively rather than as assortment of individuals. In order to achieve coordination, it is required that individuals work together towards common goals for which they need to be motivated.

◆ **Defining Authority:** The authority of sales executives should be properly defined whether it is line, staff or functional. The line authority has the power of getting things done from those lower in the hierarchy. The staff authority has suggestive power where method of implementation can be suggested by them. Functional authority is specific and limited and enables specialists in particular cases like service of technical product.

◆ **Executive Time Economisation:** Additional subordinates are added on increase in number and complexity of operations of sales department. This allows more delegation of authority by higher ranking executives. This leads to effective use of specialisations with more time spent on planning rather than operations. Top executives also need to be aware of the activities associated with routine tasks. However, with increase in number of subordinates more effort should be made for the task coordination.

DEVELOPING A SALES ORGANISATION

The five major steps included in setting up a sales organisation are:

◆ Objective definition.

◆ Demarcation of important activities.

◆ Grouping activities into positions or jobs.

◆ Assigning individuals to positions.

◆ Overseeing control and coordination.

Objective Definition

The initial step in setting up a sales organisation is to define the objectives. Generally, the long-term objectives are defined by the top management.

Demarcation of Important Activities

Important activities can be demarcated by analysis of qualitative and quantitative objectives of the sales department.

Grouping Activities into Positions or Jobs

After the identification of important activities, it is required that these activities are assigned to different personnel.

Assigning Individuals to Positions

This step requires the assignment of personnel to specific positions. This provides two choices whether to fill positions from available pool of individuals or to hire new employees.

Overseeing Control and Coordination

Executives having line authority require individuals to report to them for which they should have coordination and control capabilities. The coordination and control are possible through both formal and informal means. Informal basis of control and coordination is mostly used by strong leaders. On the other hand, the most formal form of control is the job description which is a written document. A proper job description provides accurate information regarding the role of personnel.

ISSUES IN DEVELOPING A SALES ORGANISATION

Formal and Informal Organisation

The formal organisation is developed by the management. It has a rigid structure and reporting system which often results in poor communication. Whereas, informal organisation does not have a rigid structure and reporting lead to informal organisation. Informal organisation is the counterpart of formal organisation which helps in communicating information in the form of grapevine. Without the support of informal organisation, all formal organisations would remain ineffective.

Horizontal and Vertical Organisation

A salesforce can have either a horizontal or a vertical format. In a vertical sales organisation, the structure is represented as shown in Figure 5.1.

In a vertical sales organisation, all layers report vertically as there are several layers includes in this type of sales management.

The other type is the horizontal sales organisation. The number of levels is reduced in this type of structure, but number of managers is increased. There might be seven or eight district sales managers instead of just two or three.

Span of control is a factor that is used to determine whether a horizontal or vertical organisation structure is employed. Span of control refers to "the number of employees who report to the next higher level in the organisation". Vertical organisation exists where close managerial supervision is required, whereas horizontal structure exists where wider span of control is required.

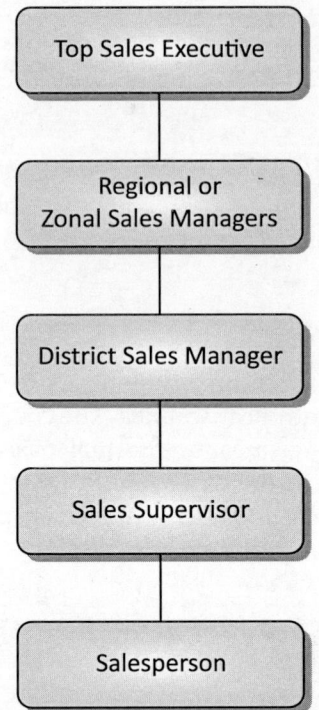

Figure 5.1 Vertical Organisations

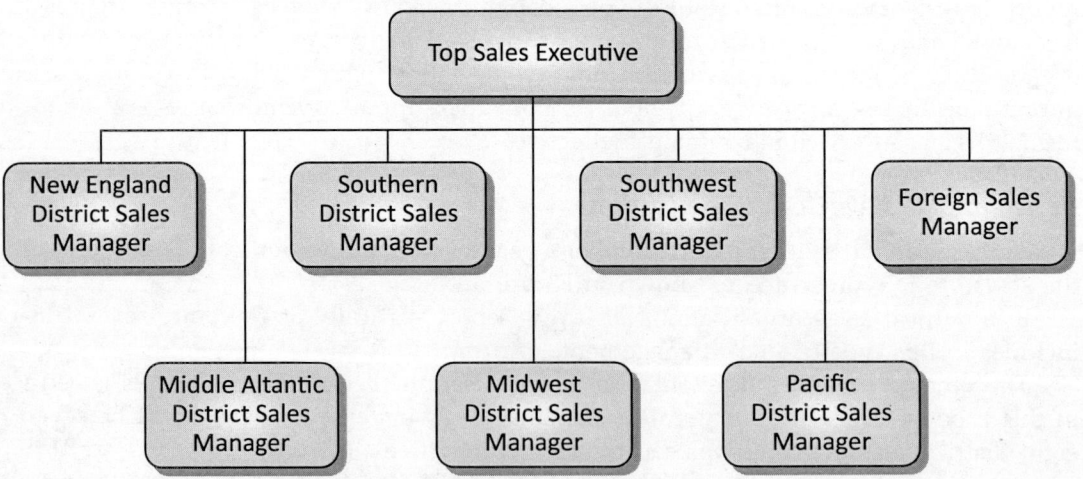

Figure 5.2 Horizontal Organisations

Centralised and Decentralised Organisations

In a centralised system, various activities like evaluation, compensation, training and recruitment are all managed from a centrally located headquarter. On the other hand, in a decentralised organisation most of the functions are performed by field sales manager. The centralisation or decentralisation also depends on the competitive necessities, cross effectiveness and size of operation. Branch offices usually emerge when the size of the operation increases. There are several advantages of a decentralised sales force which include:

1. Increased sales productivity, improved supervision and effective control.
2. Increased morale and motivation of the sales force.
3. A good training ground through a well-managed channel structure.
4. Reduction in allowances and travelling expenses.
5. Better provision for customer services due to effective control of sales personnel.
6. Intensive cultivation of the market.
7. Fixed costs are covered due to increased sales volume.
8. Line and staff components of organisations.

As the size of the operation grows it results in the staff and line sales organisation structure. Specialist in their own field is known as staff and these specialisations may include sales personnel development, sales promotion, planning dealer relations, sales analysis, service and sales training. Managing Director usually heads an organisation who has regional and staff managers as his line managers. Facilitation of customer service sales promotion and feeding in information is the job of the customer service manager. Sales promotion function and other advisory functions related to it are performed by sales promotion manager. The line managers who are responsible for controlling their own field staff and for operating results in their own territories are known as regional managers. There is a common problem of coordination of reports in the line and staff. Staff may sometimes take over the responsibility of issuing direction and orders. This problem may only be overcome when responsibility and authority is written down specially otherwise there may be dual subordination.

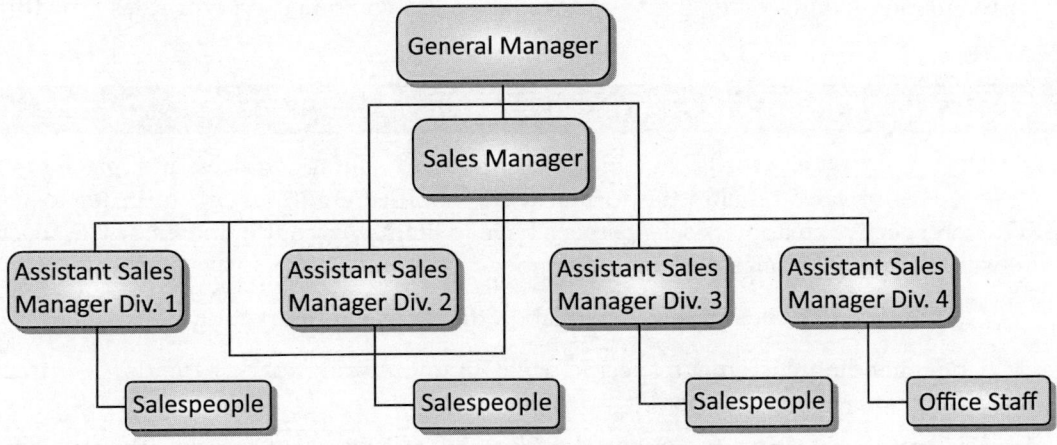

Figure 5.3 Line Organisation

TYPES OF SALES ORGANISATION STRUCTURE

Geographic Sales Organisations

Designing an organisation on the basis of geographic territory is the simplest method. For assigning a supervisor, several areas are combined together to form a territory. The sales manager is assigned territories like north, south, east and west. The sales force remains close to the customer and travel time is limited in such designs.

Product Sales Organisations

A design on the basis of type of product is preferred by organisations with a diversified product portfolio. Selling all the products of a firm is difficult on the part of the salesperson. Salespeople are recruited on the basis of their specialisation in a particular product line. Since separate salesperson is recruited for reach product line, such organisations are expensive.

Market Sales Organisations

Organisations can also be designed on the basis of profile of customers. Modern sales firm are shifting from a product-based structure to market-based structure. This type of marketing is also called vertical marketing. When the nature and type of customers is different this type of organisation is advisable.

Combination Sales Organisations

A combination of different levels of hierarchy is required in large and complex organisations. The combination could be of market, geography, function and product. Organisation serving extensive market having diversified product range use combined type of sales structure.

FIELD SALES ORGANISATION

Field sales or, in other words, outside sales refers to selling services and products by representatives of sales outside the formal team or office environment. In order to meet with the prospective customers salespersons have to literally go out in the field. The specific responsibilities of field sales personnel include:

- Help in brand development by collaborating with the marketing department.

- Understanding customer's specific needs by monitoring market trends, new trends and company's competitors.

- Presenting products to potential clients by building connections through trade shows and conferences.

- Keeping records of customer accounts and sales leads.
- Updating terms of contract with present and potential clients.
- Providing tutorials and demos to educate potential clients.
- Initiating regular meetings with current clients for nurturing relationships.
- Conducting face to face meeting with customers.

Number of Salespeople

After deciding the structure of the salesforce, the next step is to decide its size. The three approaches used for deciding the size of the salesforce are as follows:

1. **Affordability Method:** By bringing a balance between number of people required to call targeted prospects and existing customers, the size of the salesforce can be decided.

   For example, Gateway Corporation located in Mumbai has a sales target of ₹20 lacs. There was allocation of 10 per cent towards field sales force. 15 per cent of the expenses go towards supervisory expenses and average expenses of salesperson will be ₹17,000 pa.

   So, according to 15 per cent supervisory expenses, it will be expense of ₹30000 leading to a total budget of ₹1,70,000. Since, expense per staff is ₹17000, the total number of salespeople required will be 170000/17000 = 10.

2. **Incremental Method:** This method is usually followed in firms that over the period of time have been well established in the market and have a good organisational design. Generally, sales are generated from existing markets. The point where gross profit from additional sales is exceeded by costs of the staff is monitored by organisations to judge the sales performance. When the marginal response rates are positive then analysis of costs can be made to determine the number of salespeople.

3. **Workload Method:** This is the most popular method for deciding the sales force size. Call norm is where "the frequency and the number of calls a salesperson has to make are decided". Suppose a salesperson makes an average of 5 calls for selling a product. Another estimate suggests that 10 calls per day are made by a salesperson in a month. If a company wants to achieve a target of 3000 units, then a total of 3000 × 5 = 15000 calls are to be made. Since, a salesperson makes 10 calls in a day, 250 in a month and 3000 in a year, company recruits 15000/3000 = 5 people.

$$\text{Number of salespeople} = \frac{\begin{array}{c}(\text{No of existing customers} \times \text{Number of potential customers} \\ \times \text{Ideal frequency of calls} \times \text{Length of call})\end{array}}{\text{Ideal selling time for salesperson}}$$

CASE STUDY

A large company which produced personal and health care products is selling all over India. They are controlling the sales by having a geographical sales organisation as follows:

- Regional Sales Manager North
- Regional Sales Manager South
- Regional Sales Manager East
- Regional Sales Manager West

All these Managers have to report to the National Sales Manager who controls all the sales. The weekly reports are also analysed at the Centre. A sales representative, field sales supervisor and area sales manager work under the regional sales manager. This company is faced with the problem of training, recruitment and coordination of the salesman. The salesman is generally of two categories dealing with personal and health care products. These two salesmen are selling different products in the same region. This caused resentment among the customers because their time was wasted in attending to different salesman.

As all the planning is done at the centre, many problems are faced by the regional manager. Therefore, different types of salesmen are required who can understand the customers. For promotional sales this is an important consideration.

Questions

1. Can you modify the existing one or suggest an alternative organisational structure.
2. How can you further help the organisation for being more effective in sales?

SUMMARY

Sales organisation is the framework of relations of different people in the enterprise. Its function is to provide a flexible, economical and efficient administrative set up to ensure timely movement of products from warehouses to consumers. Importance of sales organisation can be judged through handling of personnel management tasks, reconciliation of complaints, collection of dues, handling the orders received, demand pattern for the products and plan to purchase. There are various forms in which sales organisation can exist. It can be either line or staff organisation. Further, sales organisation can exist in two forms that is horizontal or vertical sales organisation.

KEY TERMS

Horizontal organisation: Horizontal organisational structure is a flat management structure. Organisations with these structures often have few managers with many employees, and they allow employees to make decisions without needing manager approval.

Line organisation: Line organisation is the simplest framework for the whole administrative organisation. Line organisation approaches the vertical flow of the relationship.

Sales administrators: Sales Administrators act as the connecting piece between the customer and the Salesperson by doing things like processing orders, keeping track of customer information and providing post-sale customer service reports.

Sales organisation: Sales organisation is a department in company within logistics that designs the company as per the sales requirements.

Staff organisation: A "staff function" supports the organisation with specialised advisory and support functions.

Vertical organisation: Vertical organisational structure is a pyramid-like top-down management structure. These organisations have clearly defined roles with the highest level of leadership at the top, followed by middle management then regular employees.

EXERCISES

5.1   What is the importance and motivation behind sales association?

5.2   What are the means engaged with fostering a sales association?

5.3   What are the fundamental sorts of association structures?

5.4   Distinguish between and line and staff association as for sales.

5.5   What are the various issues in developing a sales organisation?

6

Management of Sales Territories and Quotas

LEARNING OBJECTIVES

LO1: To define and explain a sales territory along with the reasons for setting up sales territories

LO2: To describe the procedure for designing a sales territory

LO3 To discuss importance of sales quotas

LO4 To explain the types of sales quotas and methods for setting sales quotas

LO5: To plan the administration of sales quotas

INTRODUCTION

A sales territory confines a group of geographical areas, markets or customers. There may or may not be geographic boundaries in a territory. A sales territory represents "a group of customer accounts, an industry, a market or a specific geographical area". Territory Management includes the potential of market, number of customer accounts, the experience of the firm and market share in the territory, the capability of the salesperson and the frequency of sales call made.

It includes the following activities:

- Selling abilities
- Customer satisfaction
- Selling techniques
- Portfolio of accounts
- Territory size
- Reports
- Coverage
- Potential business
- Trade relations

REASONS FOR ESTABLISHING SALES TERRITORIES

- ◆ To benefit salespeople and the company.
- ◆ To allow better matching of salesperson and customer.
- ◆ To reduce sales expenses.
- ◆ To improve customer relations.
- ◆ To evaluate performance.
- ◆ To establish a salesperson's responsibility.
- ◆ To obtain entire coverage of the market.

Developing Territories

Territories can be formed as follows:

- ◆ Geographical location
- ◆ Industry
- ◆ Product use
- ◆ Method of buying
- ◆ Channels of distribution
- ◆ Sales of potential
- ◆ Workload in territories
- ◆ Arbitrarily
- ◆ Rational basis

PROCEDURE FOR DESIGNING SALES TERRITORIES

Select a Control Unit

- ◆ **Metropolitan Statistical Areas (MSA):** A geographic region with nearby networks have a serious level of monetary and social coordination with the core. Organisations whose MSA are too enormous to even consider filling in as an essential geological control of units manage huge number of clients in metropolitan regions. They usually relegate at least two sales people to a similar MSA. In such cases, organisations utilise either minor political division of urban communities or a group of ceaseless enumeration parcels as control units.

- ◆ **Trading Areas:** Exchanging regions depend on the regular progression of exchange. The exchanging region perceives those purchasers, retailers and wholesalers consider political limits in choosing where to purchase. It is hard to characterize trading areas, as they fluctuate from one item to another, for instance, typical work garments can be bought from even a town shop yet dress requires shops in large urban communities or regions. Size of trading areas are much smaller products purchased in routine. There may even be seasonal fluctuation in size of trading area.

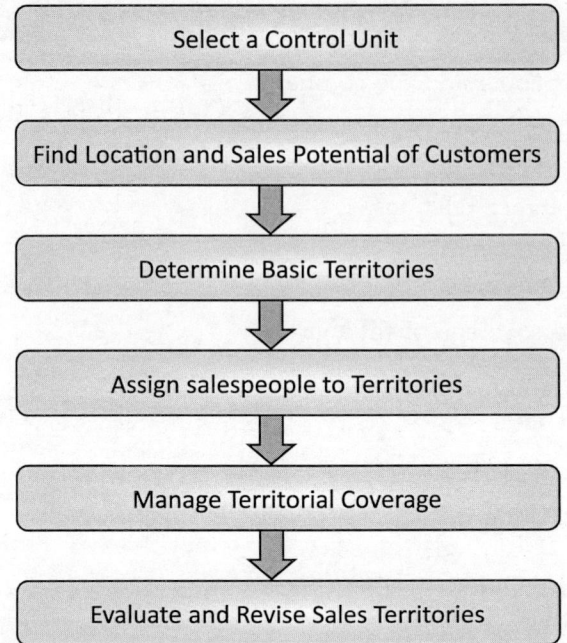

Figure 6.1   Procedure for Designing Sales Territories

♦ **States:** The state division is a reasonable option. One is the main reason for this is that the deals force is covering the market widely instead of seriously, other circumstance can be the point at which an organisation is looking for public dissemination. The fundamental trouble in involving it as a control unit is that it is a political as opposed to monetary choice.

Find Location and Sales Potential of Customers

In each control unit sales potential is determined. Each control unit is a particular geographical market segment for which the buyer must be identified precisely. Vague identification such as "our product is bought by women" is not enough but "it is bought by middle-aged, low-income women living in cities" is more precise.

Formal marketing research studies obtain identification of each possible buyer depending upon the product being marketed. After identifying potential buyers, the planner next determines the sales potential in each control unit and the market potential. Then it identifies the portion of unit market potential that the company has an opportunity to obtain.

Determine Basic Territories

The subsequent stage incorporates blend of units into 'provisional' sales domains, to get a first 'estimate' of sales regions by consolidating consistent control unit into conditional domains, each joining roughly similar deals potential. As of now number of regions are chosen accepting that all business faculty are of normal capacity. Essentially, the level of complete deals potential that the normal salesman ought to acknowledge is assessed.

Designing and Relocation of Territories

The two basic approaches for designing territories are:

1. **Market Build-up Approach:** This approach suggests that "an estimation of the present and potential products/services demand can be made by looking at how the market build-up, who are the potential users, how much they consume and at what frequency".

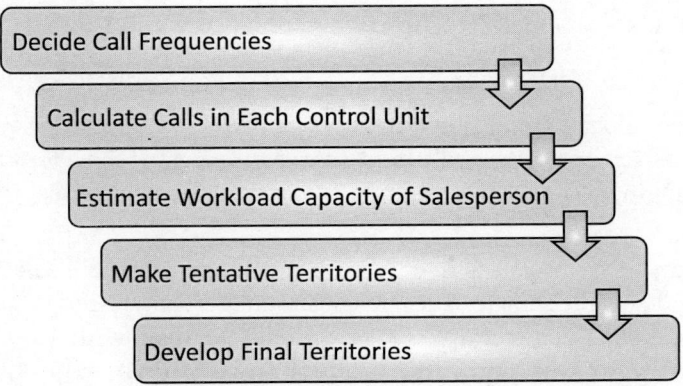

Figure 6.2   Market Build-up Approach

- ◆ *Deciding Call Frequencies:* It suggests how many times a salesperson should visit a customer in each year.
- ◆ *Calculating Calls in Each Control Unit:* Suppose the call frequency of two districts X and Y is given then the number of sales calls can be calculated by multiplying number of customers with call frequency per month.
- ◆ *Estimate Workload Capacity of Salesperson:* By multiplying the number of working days in a year with the average number of calls an estimate can be made regarding the normal workload capacity.
- ◆ *Make Tentative Territories:* The company should group adjoining control units until yearly number of calls required in that control unit equals maximum calls a salesperson can make.
- ◆ *Develop Final Territories:* By removal and addition of certain control unit's adjustments of tentative territories can be made, in cases where salesperson's workloads are not equal.

In this approach, information is gathered from trade directories or state publications which can be aggregated and consolidated to understand market potential. For example, if the market potential for cars in Tamil Nadu is 1,00,000, Bihar is 60,000 and Madhya Pradesh is 50,000, it shows that the total market potential is of 2,10,000 cars in the country. This can further be used for calculating number of salespersons required as well as total sales calls required in an area.

2. **The Workload Approach:** This approach was planned by WJ Talley based on the responsibility performed by salespersons. The accompanying advances ought to

be viewed as significant while utilising the above approach:

(i) Customers are assembled into class size as indicated by the volume of deals.

(ii) Optimum call frequencies for each class of clients are assessed.

(iii) Present and potential clients are then found geologically and organised volume wise and worth wise.

(iv) The number of present and possible clients in every volume/esteem bunch is then duplicated by the ideal call recurrence to get absolute number of arranged calls expected for each geological control unit.

Assign Salespeople to Territories

Salespeople can be allocated to sales territories once the sales territories are designed. In designing the sales territory, it is assumed that each salesperson would perform equally and have equal abilities to sell. In assigning salesperson to territories, two criteria should be considered:

♦ **Salesperson's Effectiveness in a Territory:** By comparing the salesperson's physical, cultural and social characteristics, a sales manager can easily judge the effectiveness of a salesperson. For example, it is difficult to deal with rural customers for a salesperson who was born and brought up in urban environment of Delhi or Mumbai.

♦ **Relative Ability of Salespeople:** There are certain key factors on the basis of which the relative abilities of the salesperson should be evaluated which include selling skills, ability in written and verbal communications, past performance in achieving sales quotas, market and product knowledge.

Managing Territorial Coverage

♦ **Procedure for the Development of Territories:** While creating domains a system must be followed and targets are thought of as, for example, responsibility and opportunity leveling. There are many methodologies which are quantitative in nature. The interaction starts with a specific unit of collection or base and includes specific focuses on the off chance that changes are to be made.

♦ **Objectives and Criteria for Territory Formation:** This is required because of following reasons:

(a) It affects the sales force morale and performance. Results may be measured by sales volume, market share, or profits. The job of a sales manager is to form optimum number of territories and their configuration.

(b) Another objective is the equalisation of territory potential. This is to provide equal opportunities for the sales person since territories differ in many aspects including the potential and they become big or small accordingly.

♦ **Routing the Sales Force:** Routing involves a formal pattern of travel which has to be followed by the salesperson when he/she moves through the respective territories. The order in which each segment of the territory is to be covered is reflected on a map or list.

It is the sequence of locations that are to be visited by a salesperson. The purpose of routing is more adequate coverage of market, better coordination with regional office and its requirements. More vigorous market cultivation is also part of routing.

♦ *Territory Shapes*

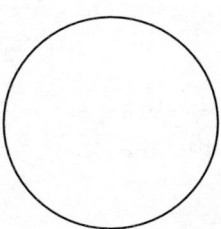 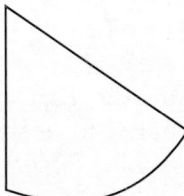 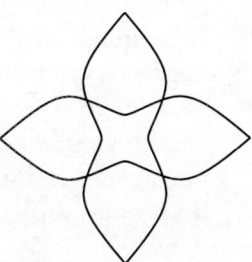

Circle
a/c distributed equally across
central part of all areas
urban areas, e.g., cars

Wedge
EMCG
Dense to rural area
less travel time

Clover leaf
Randomly distributed
careful planning to a clover
area on weekly basis

Figure 6.3 Territory Shapes

♦ **Wedge:** This is useful when areas to be covered include both urban and non-urban areas. It radiates from densely populated urban centres. Wedge can be of many sizes which are just under 360°. By balancing urban and non-urban calls, the travel time can be balanced.

♦ **Circle:** When the distribution of prospects throughout the area is even in that case this shape is appropriate. Sales person is based at the centre to ensure uniformity in the call frequency for prospects and customers.

♦ **Clover Leaf:** This pattern is adopted when accounts are randomly distributed throughout the territory. Careful planning is required so that only a week's work is enough for each leaf.

♦ **Straight Line:** This pattern of travel starts from the outer perimeter and then works backwards.

♦ **Hub and Spoke:** This is hub and spoke in place of circular pattern. Several spokes radiate from the hub in this pattern. Each calling pattern starts from the outer end of the spoke in place of circular route.

Evaluating and Revising Sales Territories

By setting up quotas, performance standards and quantitative and qualitative goals, the sales territories can be evaluated. For example, yearly, quarterly and monthly sales goals, customer satisfaction index and number of calls to be made to 'A', 'B' and 'C' type of customers located in each territory.

DEALING WITH TERRITORY MANAGEMENT PROBLEMS

Even the most carefully designed territories encounter problems. These are:

(a) **Changing Environmental Conditions:** The changing environment whether social, political or cultural has an impact on the sales territories.

(b) **Inadequate Insight into Territorial Procedures:** Sometimes the larger policies do not focus on individual problems faced within a territory which becomes difficult to manage.

(c) **Unanticipated Behaviour on the Part of the Territory Manager:** The territory manager is not always prepared to deal with every situation. In such cases also it becomes difficult to deal with problems.

SALES QUOTA

A sales quota is the sales goal set for a product line, company division or sales representative. It is primarily a managerial device for defining and stimulating sales effort.

— Philip Kotler

PURPOSE OF SALES QUOTAS

♦ **Providing Incentives on Achievement of Goals after Attaining a Particular Performance Level:** If performance is surpassed or exceeded more incentives are given. While setting quotas, it must be ensured that they are time bound, realistic, attainable, measurable and specific.

♦ **Controlling Sales Person's Activities:** It provides opportunities:

1. To take corrective actions if the salesman fails to achieve his targets,
2. For realisation of money from the account holders,
3. To plan demonstrations,
4. To gain new accounts,
5. To control the calls per day,
6. To direct and control the selling activities of sales persons,

♦ **Evaluation of Performance:** Performance against quotas also helps in performance of quantitative and qualitative activities and identifying weak and strong points of the sales person. The performance can be judged in various territories and for various products. For the satisfaction of the sales executive, a salesman may perform differently. If a sales person is below average in many ways then there is need of serious reconsideration and some action is necessary.

♦ **Control of Expenses of Sales:** For keeping the sales expenses within limits certain action is required from the sales person. Profit quotas are set by companies with the help of expense quotas. Compensation is also tied to expenses. Usually, for external factors a limit is fixed. These are—types of product, types of terrain, types of work, types of city.

♦ **Compensation Plans that are Effective:** When the quotas are achieved or exceeded then only some Indian companies give compensation. An incentive for the sales person is provided through proper compensation plans. Only when a part or full quota is achieved then some use it as a basis for bonus purposes and give bonus.

TYPES OF SALES QUOTAS

Different types of sales quotas are set by companies. Based on the level of competition, design of the organisation and business practice the method of selecting the quota is decided. Generally, there are four types of quotas which include sales volume quota, sales budget quota, sales activity quota and combination quota.

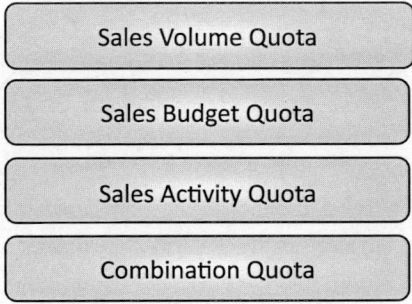

Figure 6.4 Types of Sales Quota

♦ **Sales Volume Quotas:** Sales volume quotas include product unit objectives or sales in rupees for a specific time period. For example, a car company calculates sales by number of cars sold, whereas a FMCG company may calculate the sales in rupees. Usually, such type of quotas is set for the entire year. This quota is then further sub-divided into monthly quotas of three, six or nine months.

Sales volume quotas may be set as follows:

- Sales force
- Branch offices
- Sales districts
- Sales territories
- Sales divisions
- Product range
- Product line

There are three ways in which companies set sales volume quotas:

1. **Dollars Sales Volume Quotas:** Rather than setting quotas in units, it is easier to manage in rupees or dollars when salespeople are required to sell many products. Another reason for using dollars sales volume quota is that it can be expressed in percentage as it allows an analysis of selling expenses to sales.

2. **Unit Sales Volume Quotas:** There are three situations in which companies set unit sales volume quota. One situation is when few products are being sold by the salespeople. Second is when there is rapid price fluctuation. The third is when there is high price of each product.

3. **Point Sales Volume Quotas:** It is conveyed in 'points'. When profitability of a company needs to be improved then this method is used.

♦ **Profit Quotas:** Multiproduct companies usually apply these kind of quotas as different levels of profits are provided by different products. Optimum use of time is made by salespersons which creates opportunities for them.

Product	Sales price per unit	Profit margin per unit	Volume per month	Net profit per month
Product X	₹400	₹280 (70%)	60,000	168,00,000
Product Y	₹200	₹80 (40%)	25,000	2,00,000
Product Z	₹100	₹20 (20%)	10,000	2,00,000

♦ **Expense Quotas:** Selling costs within reasonable limits are related to expense quotas. Expenses linked to different levels of sales attained by sales force are set by some of the companies. A percentage of the territory's sales volume is given to the salespeople as an expense budget. Only this amount is to be spent by the salesperson as expenditure.

♦ **Activities Quotas:** These quotas set objectives for job-related duties that are useful for the attainment of salespeople's performance targets. Activity quotas have long term implications on the goodwill of the firm as they make the sales force perform certain activities. A target level is usually set for measuring performance of salespersons by a sales organisation.

Common types of activity quotas include:

- Number of new accounts opened
- Number of calls made for recovery
- Numbers of dealers visited
- Number of service calls made
- Number of sales presentations made

♦ **Combination Quotas:** Quota combinations are used by many companies.Activity quota and sales volume are two of the most commonly combined quotas. Both selling and non-selling activities are influenced by these quotas. The salespeople might get confused of too many quotas applied. Quotas should be applied on the basis of products that result in maximum sales, total sales volume and other important activities.

ADMINISTRATION OF QUOTA SYSTEM

♦ **Quotas Should be Attainable, Fair and Accurate:** A function of the quota setting procedure is to obtain accurate quotas. Accurate quotas result from skillful blending of operating and planning information with sound judgement. Determining the proper blend of sales potential and previous experience helps in setting a fair quota.

♦ **Maintaining and Securing Acceptance from Sales Personnel:** Management must ensure that a sales personnel understands setting procedure and quotas. Securing staff acceptance of quotas is a critical step to convey this understanding. If sales personnel are not able to understand the procedures used in establishment of quotas, they may suspect, e.g., that the quotas are a technique to obtain extra effort from them at no cost to the company.

♦ **Sales Personnel Participation:** The process is simplified, if sales personnel participate in quota setting, the task of explaining quotas and how they are determined. Some sales force participation can obtain more accurate and realistic quotas but it is not advisable to turn the whole quota setting over to sales staff.

♦ **Informative Sales Personnel:** Sales personnel are kept informed of their progress relative to quotas in an effective sales management. Frequent reports are received by sales personnel giving details of their performance to date. Analysis of their own strong and weak points and taking corrective action is permitted through this way.

♦ **Continuous Review and Control by Management:** For the administration of the quota system, there is a need for continuous monitoring of performance. Performance statistics should be analysed with minimum delay and arrangements must be made together.

LIMITATIONS OF SALES QUOTAS

♦ Quotas are not helpful in situations where goods are in shortage.

♦ Generally, quotas are set at higher levels.

♦ Getting reliable sales estimates from the market is not easy.

♦ Some kinds of sales quotas are difficult to understand by salesman.

CASE STUDY

Hewlett Packard is a Palo Alto-based, global company with a portfolio spanning from IT infrastructure, services, software, personal systems and printing. In order to achieve long term profitable growth and transform the company, a multi-year initiative has been embarked upon. One of the key elements of HP's dramatic transformation was increase in sales performance as the company had a sales team of 30,000 sales representatives selling over 150 product lines. HP took the help of Anaplan in order to improve effectiveness and visibility of territory and quota planning process. Anaplan is the leading planning and performance management platform for smart businesses. Anaplan combines cloud collaboration, predictive analytics and unrivalled planning and modeling engine, into one simple interface for business users. Anaplan is a privately held company based in San Francisco with 16 offices worldwide.

Before implementing Anaplan, there was a gap between the design and implementation of their annual sales territory and quota assignments. "Before Anaplan, we were always looking at what actually got deployed in a rearview mirror," said Sue Barsamian, Senior Vice President, Worldwide Indirect Sales, HP Enterprise Group, Hewlett-Packard. "This was a spreadsheet-run exercise, and by the time that all got rolled back up, and people corrected minor errors along the way, we were usually at the beginning of Q2."

"To attack this problem, we were beginning to develop a solution in-house because we really didn't see anything in the marketplace until we came across Anaplan," said Rob Ficalora, Senior Director, IT, Hewlett-Packard. "The capabilities that we could get with Anaplan, frankly, exceeded our expectations and our own requirements for building a homegrown solution. It gave us an opportunity to stretch beyond the ideas that we had for quota deployment."

"With Anaplan, we moved entirely away from this being a rearview mirror conversation," said Barsamian. "We don't even go live until we're sure that our design is being deployed as expected and that we are comfortable with the way that quota is actually rolled out. I have been at HP eight years, and I have never seen a start of a year like we had this year, thanks to Anaplan."

"With Anaplan, we made it easier to deploy coverage and quota with complete transparency, improving sales target and performance" said Slaby. "I see all kinds of opportunities with Anaplan. We'll have the ability to compare plans we set in Anaplan to actual performance, build models based on best practices, create simulations that help our businesses test assumptions, and select the best plan. Anaplan will help us move the sales planning process from art to science."

Questions

1. Do you think HP made the right decision in implementing Anaplan?
2. Would you recommend any other alternative option like Anaplan for HP?

SUMMARY

A sales quota is a sales goal, sales target, or minimum sales level that a sales entity—team or individual—aims to achieve. There are five types of sales quotas—sales volume, expense, profit, activities and combination. These quotas should be applied while keeping in mind the key points of quota administration. A sales territory confines a group of geographical areas, markets, or customers. While developing territories a procedure has to be followed and objectives are considered such as work load and opportunity equalisation. There are two approaches to designing territories which include market build-up approach and workload approach.

KEY TERMS

Sales territory: A sales territory is the customer group or geographical area for which an individual salesperson or a sales team holds responsibility.

Sales quotas: A sales quota is a sales goal, sales target, or minimum sales level that a sales entity—team or individual—aims to achieve.

EXERCISES

6.1 What is a sales territory? Why do firms establish sales territories?

6.2 'Quotas' can act as a 'motivator' as well as demotivator—Comment.

6.3 What are the various types of sales quotas that are fixed for salesmen?

6.4 What is the procedure of designing the sales quotas?

6.5 Discuss the market build up approach for designing sales territories.

6.6 Give a brief account of the administration of quota system and the limitations of sales quota.

7

Staffing of Salesforce

LEARNING OBJECTIVES

LO1: To carry out recruitment and selection of the salespeople

LO2: To organise hiring and socialisation of the salespeople

INTRODUCTION

There is a strong impact on the company's profits and performance if the salesforce staffing is appropriate. The company's strategic marketing plan is carried out by the salesforce. Therefore, choosing the right people is critical for any organisation. Staffing the salesforce includes planning, recruitment, selection, hiring and socialisation is among the most challenging and important responsibilities of sales management.

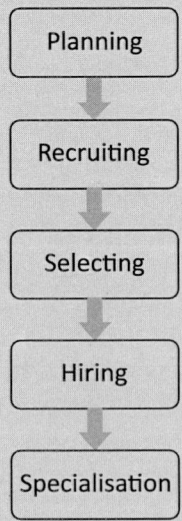

Figure 7.1 Staffing Process

PLANNING STAGE

The planning stage involves three tasks as follows:

1. **Setting Up Responsibility:** The responsibility of various activities and stages of staffing process lies with the management who must make such decisions. Most decisions are made by the head in a small organisation. However, in large and medium organisation such responsibility lies with the human resource managers.

2. **Deciding Number of Salespeople Needed:** An important part of planning is deciding how many salespeople are needed. Planning of manpower requirements needs to be done in advance by the regional and branch sales managers.

3. **Outlining Type of Salespeople Needed:** The steps involved in developing the type of salespeople needed are as follows:

   ♦ *Job Analysis:* Job analysis is the systematic collection of information on a particular sales job. The procedure developed for conducting a job analysis involves development of duties such as making sales presentations and understanding customer needs.

   ♦ *Job Description:* Job description is a written and formal statement of detailed account of job. It covers the job title, reporting relationship, types of products and services, types of customers, duties and responsibilities, job demands, key result areas and location to be covered.

   ♦ *Job Specification*: Job specifications are decided on the basis of duties and responsibilities mentioned in the job description. In order to perform well on the job, the recruit must have certain traits and skills.

RECRUITMENT OF SALESFORCE

According to Yoder "Recruitment is a process to discover the source of manpower to meet the requirements of the staffing schedule and to employ effective measures for attracting that manpower in adequate numbers to facilitate effective selection of an efficient working force."

Factors Affecting the Recruitment Policy of Sales Personnel

1. Number of volunteers
2. Recruitment sources
3. Recruitment necessities
4. Recruitment expense
5. Size of the deals association
6. Rate of turnover
7. Forecasted deals volume
8. Government strategies

9. Personnel arrangements of contending association
10. Organisational personnel policies

Sequence of Recruitment Process

Before an organisation begins the process of recruitment, a checklist of questions should be framed outlining the chronology of process:

I. What kind of job is to be filled?

For answering this question, a wide spectrum of sub-questions needs to be answered.

(a) What is the main role for this job?
Name of the job, who is the boss, why the job exists and use of money, materials and people.
(b) This job deals with which kind of buyers?
(c) Is this company looking for future area or sales manager?
(d) What kind of remuneration would be provided?

II. What person would be successful at the job?

Intellectual Abilities: The job requires creativity necessary to adapt, introduce and recognise new ideas, common sense and general intelligence.

Motivation: Determination of motivation and interests of salespersons for a particular job. The driving force is money, achievement, recognition and progress which has the most importance.

Specific Attainments: Does the job require professional/technical qualification or knowledge. Is some experience also required for the job?

People Skills: Dealing with people is very essential for a selling job. Whether the sales person has required leadership or communication skills. The kind of impact that can be made through communication skills in the mind of the consumers.

Working Conditions: Whether the recruitment and selection of a salesperson could be affected by hours of work and mobility and other related conditions.

III. Where to find such a person?

Sources for identifying potential candidates include:

Employment Agencies: These agencies perform the task, usually done by employer, like reference check and batteries of tests. A complete detail of job specifications and a clear statement of the objective of the job should be available to the employment agency.

Advertising: This is mainly done through newspaper advertising where ads appear in classifieds section or in the form of display advertisements so that the vast majority of applicants through single advertisement by the company.

Figure 7.2 Job Advertisement

Internal Transfers: The internal sources include the non-selling section of the sales department and other departments. The company policies are already familiar to the employees who desire a transfer. The aptitude for selling can be tested by trial or formal testing.

Educational Institutions: These sources include vocational institutes, technical institutes, universities and colleges. These institutions are supposed to teach them to express themselves reasonably well, reason logically and develop the ability to think.

IV. Which person should be recruited out of selected applications?

Three step approach is to be followed:

- **Comparison of Application:** Remove all who do not meet essential criteria by checking their CVs.
- **Move to the Areas Requiring "Measurement Instrument":** An assessment at interview is needed, for instance, ambitions, leisure interests, health, present financial situation, domestic and social situation, family background, work history and education.

♦ **Identification of Pattern Behaviour:** Here the stress is on the term pattern—the organisation should look for the consistent picture in social life, at work, at school for example commitment, perseverance, tenacity etc.

SELECTION PROCESS

The selection process consists of a series of steps that act like filters. The applicant may be dropped at any of these steps. The major steps in the process of selection are as follows:

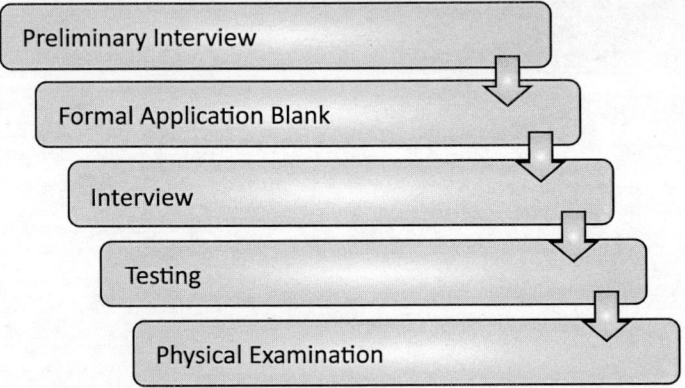

Figure 7.3   Selection Process

1. Preliminary Interview

The receptionist at the employment office usually undertakes the initial screening. Information regarding the nature of the jobs in the organisation is essentially gathered through a sorting process used in the preliminary interview. This necessary information is then asked from candidates relating to their age, physical appearance, job interest, reasons for leaving present job, salary demanded, skill, experience and education. A candidate is eliminated at the preliminary stage if he does not meet the criteria.

2. Formal Application Blank

A brief history sheet regarding the employee's background is called an application blank that if need arises can be used for future reference. It is a widely accepted device for gathering information from prospective applicants. This helps the management in making proper selection. By indicating the areas of interest, this application blank provides preliminary information for conducting the interview.

Standard application form uses:

♦ **Personal Information:** Name, address, gender, marital status, children, date of birth
♦ **Education:** Membership of professional bodies, specified training, qualifications, higher education, schooling.

♦ **Employment History:** Positions, duties, responsibility, duration, dates of employment, name of companies, number of jobs held.

♦ **Other Interests:** Membership of societies, hobbies and sports.

3. Interview

In order to consider the suitability of a candidate for a job under consideration an attempt is made to gather relevant information which forms part of the interview. This is a satisfactory method for judging the attitude towards selling, personal appearance and oral communication of candidates.

♦ **Interview Decisions:** The following important decisions need to be taken regarding the interviews.

When: At the initial stage of screening usually a short interview is used, whereas an in-depth or detailed interview is used in the selection process at a later stage.

Where: Similarly place for interview depends upon degree of decentralisation and size of the organisation. In highly decentralised organisations the responsibility lies with the regional/branch/district level sales department.

Who: These usual practice is to evaluate each person by interviewing several of the applicants. In small organisations this responsibility lies with the top personnel of the marketing and sales department whereas in highly decentralised and large organisations the responsibility lies with the branch or district sales manager.

♦ **Interviewing Techniques:** There are four types of interviewing techniques. These include the following:

Non-directed/ Non-structured Interview: Instead of following a standard format of questions, a relaxed form of discussion takes place. Maximum insight regarding a person's interests and attitudes is gained through non-directive techniques.

Patterned/ Structured Interview: In this type of interview, a prepared list of questions is given to the interviewers or designing a specific outline of questions for eliciting a basic core of information.

Stress Interview: It is a complex form of interview. A hostile role is assumed towards the applicant by the interviewer. By frustrating, embarrassing and annoying him; the interviewer puts the applicant on the defensive.

Rating Scales: In this method of interview, different interviewers rate the individual on the same rating scale to get comparable results. For example, an interviewer is forced to choose from one of the following answers in order to evaluate the attitude of the candidate: loyalty, positivity, health, pessimistic, complaining, negative.

4. Testing

"Tests are the most misused, the least understood, yet the most valuable sources of information about the applicants".

A psychological test can be defined as "Systematic approach for comparing the behaviour of two or more persons". In general sense, "It is a sample of an aspect of an individual's behaviour, performance or attitude".

Different Types of Psychological Tests

Aptitude or Ability Test: The ability of a candidate to learn a skill or job is measured by assessing the ability or talent of the candidate. The attention is focused on a particular talent type: mechanical bend of mind, reasoning or learning. These tests include the following types:

(i) *Mental or Intelligence Test:* This test measures the intelligence quotient or intellectual activity of the candidate. They determine the candidate's spatial visualisation, speed of perception, inductive reasoning, memory and word fluency.

(ii) *Mechanical Aptitude Test:* These tests measure a person's visual-motor integration or coordination by measuring the capacity of the individual to learn a particular type of mechanical work.

(iii) *Psychomotor or Skill Test:* The ability of a person to do a specific job is measured by these tests. These tests measure coordination, control, muscular movement, motor ability and mental dexterity.

Personality Test: These tests try to find maturity and characteristic mood, emotional reactions and individual's value systems. These tests have the following categories:

(i) *Situation Tests:* These tests reveal the ingenuity of a person under pressure and the ability of a person to undergo stress.

(ii) *Objective Tests:* These tests measure self-confidence, dominance-submission, self-sufficiency and neurotic tendencies.

(iii) *Project Tests:* A person's personality, motives and values are reflected through his interpretation of certain standard stimulus situations.

Figure 7.4 Psychological Test

Achievement Test: An individual's knowledge about a subject is determined through achievement tests. These tests determine the capability of an individual.

(i) *Job Knowledge Measurement Tests:* These are administered for determining the feasibility to perform the job and degree of their qualification.

(ii) *Work Sample Tests:* The actual job is to be performed as a test.

Interest Test: Based on the relationship between motivation and test, there exists the interest tests. Hence, to be more successful a person should have greater interest in the job besides having the required ability.

5. Physical Examination

The job of a salesperson requires tolerance for hard working conditions, strength, and unusual stamina. The major purpose of physical examination is:

(i) The existing disabilities of the candidates are discovered through this mode.

(ii) People who suffer from contagious diseases are rejected from the process.

(iii) The indication of whether the candidate can physically perform the job of the salesperson is provided through this method.

6. Reference Check

References are given of those people who can be relied upon to give positive feedback. The main role of reference checks is to verify facts like the nature of the past selling job, absenteeism, sales volume, earnings, dates of employment. The most common way of checking reference is by letter, telephone or personal visit.

HIRING STAGE

In order to give a positive impression to the candidates, the hiring process should be implemented properly where people can feel their importance.

Employment Offer

A candidate who successfully passes through all the preceding steps is extended the offer of employment. The key contents of the job offer include compensation, responsibilities and designation.

Rating of Interviewee

The various facts should be noted and compared with the requirement. The ranking should be provided as follows:

1. Perfect match
2. Average match

3. Below average

4. Totally unsatisfactory

For arriving at the final recommendation, the scores should not be averaged or totalled as the weighing for the different factors varies. What must be done by the manager is consideration of a mixture of factors and identification of weak and strong points. A four-category scale is used for this purpose. Jobs are offered immediately to people of category 1. Those who are not qualified in all respects but are still worth employing are offered jobs in category 2. Category 3 men are taken only in dire circumstances when it is mandatory to employ someone. But however desperate the manager is, he should not employ people in category 4.

Placement of Sales Personnel

After an offer of employment has been accepted and the final stage in procurement function is concluded, then comes the process of placing the individual and orienting him to the organisation.

Placement may be defined as "the determination of the job to which an accepted candidate is to be assigned and his assignment to the job. It is a matching of what the supervisor has reason to think he can do with the job demands, it is a matching of what he imposes and what he offers in the form of payroll, companionship with others, promotional possibilities etc."

Probation

The employee is usually put on a probation period, of around 2 years after which his employment may be regularised. Only rarely the employee is asked to quit, that too in extremely serious circumstances. Until the trial period is over, the employee is placed as a probationer.

SOCIALISATION

The staffing process becomes complete once the assimilation and socialisation activities are complete. Socialisation is the process through which the new salespersons learn values, norms, attitudes and behaviour of people who are already working in the organisation. The task of introducing the new environment and new job to the salespeople is done through this. New employees may leave the company soon if the task of socialising is not successful.

Future Possibilities

A company must look into its future requirements beforehand so that it does not fall short of the needs of a salesman. Therefore, two different types of profiles are required when filling similar positions. Generally, people having the ability to accept responsibility, self-reliance and leadership have management potential as opposed to career sales staff. People tend to become frustrated and leave the job unless different standards are adopted. On the other hand, there will be no potential management pool if only men with career salesman potential are appointed.

"Why 2 out of 5 salespersons left within 6 months of joining the company?", asked marketing manager of Jetflow Ltd. "I think, there may be something wrong with our staffing process," responded Ashok Singh, the sales manager without knowing the real reasons for the turnover of salespeople.

Jetflow Ltd. started marketing and manufacturing consumer durable products like table fans for business customers and household customers in 2015. The marketing office was located in Delhi, the capital of India. Jetflow was a newly established company and for its first year of operations, the company decided to recruit twenty salespersons for covering major metros and cities near the National Capital Region. The staffing process included deciding the job qualifications of salespersons. Advertisements were placed in the local newspapers by the administration manager. The resumes of applicants were forwarded to Ashok Singh, who screened the same and sent interview calls to about 40 applicants. The initial interviews were conducted by Ashok Singh and the final interviews of the applicants that were short-listed were conducted by marketing manager. The appointment letters were issued to the selected candidates. Some of the candidates had a problem as the company policy did not provide consideration for providing a suitable residence. Ashok Singh conducted one-week training programme and generally guided the new salespersons, who reported to him directly.

There was a delay in the receipt of new fans from the factory located at Gurgaon in Haryana. During this period of 6 months, Ashok Singh was asked to conduct market surveys and to look after the marketing communications function of the entire group of companies. He asked the salespersons for a collection of information on various prospective new products like power tillers and water purifiers in which the group was considering the possibilities of investments in future.

During this period, 2 salespersons suddenly stopped coming to work, after collecting their salaries of the previous working months.

Questions

1. What might be the reasons for 2 out of 5 salespersons leaving the company within a year of joining?
2 What improvements do you suggest in the staffing process followed by the company?
3. Was Ashok Singh right in getting market surveys done by the new salespersons?

SUMMARY

"Recruitment is a process to discover the source of manpower to meet the requirements of the staffing schedule and to employ effective measures for attracting that manpower in adequate numbers to facilitate effective selection of an efficient working force."Before an organisation begins the process of recruitment, a checklist of questions should be framed outlining the chronology of process. The selection refers to choosing the right candidates from the pool of eligible candidates to fill the vacant job positions in the organisation. After an offer of employment has been accepted and the final stage in procurement function is concluded, then comes the process of placing the individual and orienting him to the organisation.

KEY TERMS

Placement: Placement is the process of assigning a specific job to each one of the selected candidates.

Recruitment: Recruitment refers to the overall process of identifying, sourcing, screening, shortlisting, and interviewing candidates for jobs within an organisation.

Selection: The selection refers to choosing the right candidates from the pool of eligible candidates to fill the vacant job positions in the organisation.

EXERCISES

7.1 How does mental testing assist in picking and correcting contenders for the right work?

7.2 What are the different sorts of meeting strategies? Portray them momentarily.

7.3 What are the means engaged with determination framework?

7.4 The choice of sales rep shifts from one organisation to another, from one item to another and from one market to another. Make sense of with the assistance of model.

7.5 Discuss the importance of the socialisation stage in staffing process.

8

Training the Salesforce

LEARNING OBJECTIVES

LO1: To know the stages of a person's career cycle

LO2: To discuss how to design a sales training programme

LO3: To understand the sales training process

INTRODUCTION

The demand of value conscious customers must be met by today's salespeople. Organisations will be in constant need of training programmes as long as businesses strive to improve, new people enter the workforce and technology changes. The concept remains the same even if the term "training" may change. Also, it is important for the people to adjust their attitudes, applying new knowledge and mastering new skills with changing environment and demand.

STAGES OF A PERSON'S CAREER CYCLE

Preparation

Orientation and training should be emphasised for the salesperson. At this stage it is important to know about the basic selling techniques and instructions. The salesperson should know about the products he has to sell, should have knowledge about the company and understand the environment in which he has to function.

Development

The salesperson should be provided field coaching along with supervision. The salesman becomes productive during the second stage. He should be able to identify problems. The salesperson should not acquire bad habits.

Maturity

The salesperson uses a "smarter than harder" work formula. There is a requirement for refresher training at this stage. They can be promoted to more responsible positions, transferred to new territories/areas and also given new challenges. Career plateauing takes place sometimes due to inadequate training. Development and growth are hampered due to lack of relevant training.

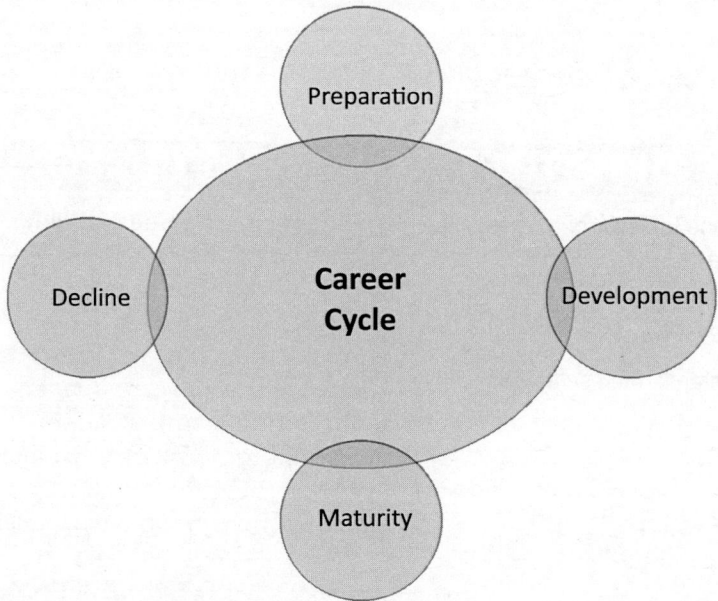

Figure 8.1 Stages of Career Cycle

Decline

The salesperson becomes problematic and requires motivational training. The productivity of the salesman is difficult to avert and decreases considerably. The effects of detraining are offset by training imparted at proper time.

DESIGNING THE SALES TRAINING PROGRAMME

Aim of Training

♦ **Identifying Initial Training Needs:** For identifying initial training needs of sales training programme there is requirement of analysing three main factors:

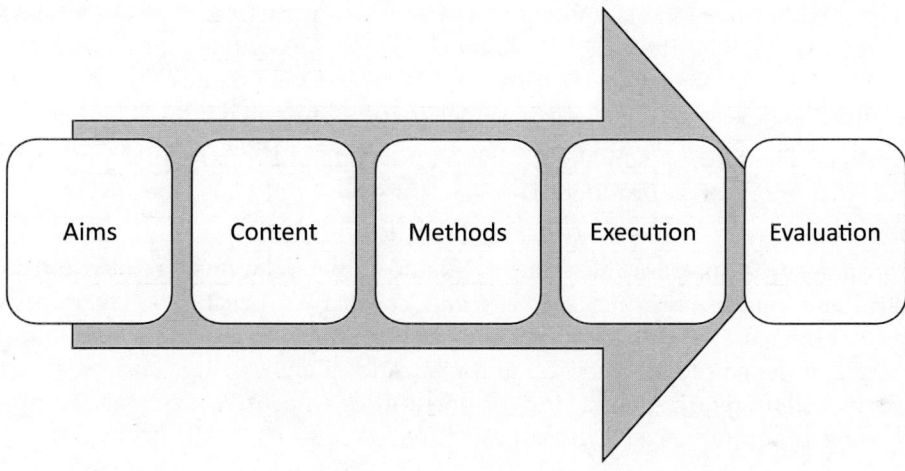

Figure 8.2   AC MEE Decisions

 (i) *Job specification:* The job specification gives details of the qualifications needed to perform a job.

 (ii) *Background and experience of the trainee:* The points on which new personnel are most likely to need training are provided in the set of job specifications.

(iii) *Marketing policies related to sales:* The amount of training needed is understood by the gap between the qualifications a trainee already has and those mentioned in the job specifications. But setting training precisely according to individual differences is not practically possible.

(iv) *Identification of continuous sales training programmes:* To determine initial sales training needs it is important to analyse the sales related marketing policies as difference in training programme is determined by difference between policies, selling practices, markets and products.

 ♦ **Continuing Sales Training Programmes:** It means due to changes in sales personnel, organisation, marketing policies, product and market; the needs of experienced sales personnel are understood.

Content of Training

For all the sales training programmes, the content of training is not the same. It varies from company to company due to different organisational size, experience, trainee's ability, company policies, markets and products. Generally sales training programme comprises of following areas:

 ♦ **Product Data:** The nature of the product helps to decide the type of training that is to be provided. In case the product is non-technical, then a minimum amount of training is required, however for highly technical products most of the training programme focuses on the product training.

♦ **Sales Technique:** In this context two views are provided. First view states that a product will sell easily if the salesman has reasonable intelligence, good voice, good appearance and attractive personality. The other view states that basic training is required for every new sales personnel that is appointed.

♦ **Markets:** The salesperson should have knowledge of a particular product, location and customers of a product. The salesperson should also be aware of financial conditions, motives and buying habits of the customers.

♦ **Company Information:** Information like customer relations, credit extension, spare parts and repairs, product services and company's pricing policy is provided to the salesperson of the company. Further for job effectiveness and boosting the morale of the employee, medical and insurance plans, savings and retirement plans, advancement requirements and opportunities, incentive systems, compensation, training programmes, selection procedure.

Methods of Training

Based on the content of the training, appropriate training method is selected from the following:

♦ **Lecture:** The instructions provided by a trainer to trainees to increase their knowledge is called lecture method. In this method trainees generally listen and watch however some forms of lectures allow questioning also. In comparison to other methods this one is more economical. If the initial training is brief, then this method is best for covering the desired training content.

Figure 8.3   Lecture Method

♦ **Personal Conference:** This is an informal and unstructured method of training. Depending on the topics discussed and personalities of the trainer and trainee, there is variation in the personal conference.

♦ **Demonstration:** In this method the salesman silently observes the sales manager as he carries out the real selling call on a prospect or customer. For the training of new salespersons, this is the most appropriate method.

◆ **Role Playing:** In this form of training, firstly the trainer describes the situations and personalities involved in training. Role playing is defined as "a method of human interaction which involves realistic behaviour in an imaginary situation".

The merits of role playing include: emphasis on learning by doing. Immediate knowledge of the results. Stress on human sensitivity and interactions. High interest and involvement of trainees.

◆ **Case Discussion:** An oral, written or fictional set of data forms part of a case. As part of a trainee, the miniature summary and description dealing with solutions or actions regarding various issues and problems. When cases are analysed, trainees are given problems to be identified and through group discussions they need to find solutions.

◆ **Gaming Simulation:** This method is quite similar to role playing. It has a unique feature that it uses contrived situations and highly structured situations based on which feedback is received by players. As participants involve themselves in game play, they are easily able to learn.

◆ **On-the-job Training:** Here special training instructors, supervisors or skilled co-workers train and coach the salesman. The job is meant by practice and personal observation. There are three steps in this method. First, particular selling situations are described by experienced sales person. Next, the coach makes the actual sales call in the presence of the trainees. Lastly, the trainee makes the sales call in the supervision of the coach followed by appraisal and discussion.

◆ **Programmed Learning:** A sequence of steps is followed in programmed instruction where the central panel of an electronic computer acts as a guide in the performance of a service of operation or desired operation. Due to several constraints and high cost of operation, programmed instructions have not been widely adopted for sales training.

Figure 8.4 Programmed Learning

♦ **Correspondence Courses:** To acquaint people with new product development and applications, correspondence courses are used by experienced sales person in companies that are small and have highly technical products but have widely deployed salesforce.

Execution of Sales Training

It involves the decision making regarding following four key questions:

1. **Who will be the trainees?**

    The criteria for identifying trainees includes:

    (a) Seniority for example for greater seniority the greater will be the opportunity.

    (b) Convenience of trainer and trainee.

    (c) Punishment for poor performance.

    (d) Reward for good performance.

2. **Who will be the trainers?**

    Training provided by trainers during different phases include:

    (a) *Sales Training Staff:* In large organisations reporting to the top sales executive is done by the sales training director. Some part of the training is given by the district sales manager and some training is given by the director himself. On the other hand, in small organisations, assistant sales managers perform this task.

    (b) *Continuing Sales Training:* The top sales executive has the responsibility of continuing sales training. For executing the sales training programme, the need and design are recognised by the top sales executive.

    (c) *Initial Sales Training:* If the initial sales training is a staff function, then the responsibility is given to the personnel director but if this is a line function then the training is assigned to the top sales executive.

    (d) *Outside Experts:* Portions of sales training programmes relating to sales techniques like prospecting, telephone are conducted with the help of outside experts.

3. **When the training will take place?**

    (a) *Initial Sales Training Programmes:* There are several factors like management plans for changing sales force size, turnover, sales personnel and size of sales force which impact the number of new personnel trained each year which in turn influences the timing for initial sales training. Training programmes are infrequent when a small number of sales persons are recruited. On the other hand, training programmes are scheduled several times a year when a large number of sales persons are recruited.

    (b) *Continuing Sales Training Programmes:* Learning must be continuous in an effective sales training programme. In the light of new developments, some concepts must be modified and others must be assimilated.

Retraining helps in following:

(a) To overcome the forgetful tendency of human brain

(b) New selling aids

(c) New customer problem

(d) New product applications

(e) New refinements of selling techniques

4. **Where will the training site be?**
   At centralised or decentralised points, the training programmes are held. Higher costs are incurred in bringing trainees to the central point in the centralised programme. There are serious defects in decentralised training. Without the supervision of top management decentralised training cannot be executed. Hence, the top management should adopt a centralised and decentralised mode of training.

Evaluation of Training Programmes

This may be the last step of the training programme but still it is very important. Evaluation includes the comparison of the training programme's aim with the outcomes.

♦ Market share percentages

♦ Written tests

♦ Observers which work with sales personnel

Stages of a person's career cycle check the sequence in contents

CASE STUDY

The Walking Company aims to improve customer's lives, on a promise that may be perceived as a lofty customer experience. They want people to walk out of their stores with a changed experience of buying a pair of shoes using personalized comfort, fit and service.

This is being successfully done by them. As recently reported by Forbes, leading comfort shoe brands are sold by the company and it differentiates itself from others by focussing on offering "experiential retail". In order to deliver customized service based on the individual needs of footwear, sales person is trained so that every customer feels that the experience is unique to their expectations. Consistently, the training that is outcome driven is the key for ensuring that this happens homogeneously across the 200 stores throughout the United States.

Further, the retailer is taking retail sales training to new heights by using gamification for increase in performance, retention and employee engagement.

A behaviour-based training model is applied by the company, which relies heavily on gamification to reward employees with points when they participate in learning activities and translation of that knowledge into new behaviours. For example, sales person receive points when they engage with the training content which can then be redeemed for the prizes. This incentive has led to the transformation of disenfranchised employees into sales superstars. They look forward to new modules of training and how it benefits companies and their customers.

Questions

1. Discuss how the sales training methods of the Walking Company have helped in satisfying its customers.
2. Identify some other unique methods of training used by other companies.

SUMMARY

Organisations will be in need of training as long as businesses strive to improve, new people enter the workforce and technology changes. For all the sales training programmes, the content of training is not the same. It varies from company to company due to different organisational size, experience, trainee's ability, company policies, markets and products. Based on the content of the training, appropriate training methods are selected. There are various methods of training—lecture, conference, demonstration, role playing, case discussion, game simulation, programmed learning and correspondence courses.

KEY TERMS

Career cycle: The lifecycle of the employee-employer relationship beginning with one's awareness of the organisation through their employment at the organisation to the exit from the organisation.

On the job training: On-the-job training is when employees observe the processes and procedures that their employer uses to create an efficient and effective workplace.

Off the job training: Off-the-job training refers to an education method where employees learn more about their job or the latest advancements in their field at a location away from their workplace.

Sales training: Sales training is an organised activity involving fact finding, planning, coaching, practicing and purposive attempts to develop selling skill and to add these skills to selected native ability, casually acquired knowledge and experience.

EXERCISES

8.1 How should a proper training programme be executed and evaluated?

8.2 What are the various methods of training a salesman?

8.3 The aim of training is to make the sales person more competent to the assigned job. How will you identify the training needs of a salesman?

8.4 Describe the different stages of a salesperson's career cycle.

8.5 Give detailed description of the contents of a training programme.

9

Motivating the Salesforce

INTRODUCTION

There are several ways of defining motivation like "the psychological aspect which helps the salesman to a goal directed behaviour". The main motive of motivation is aiding the salesman in satisfying their goals for improving their work efficiency by stimulation.

The main objectives of motivation are:

1. The achievement of sales targets through cooperation of salesmen.
2. Maintenance of high morale among salesmen.
3. Establishment of cordial relationship between managers and salesmen.
4. Stimulation of salesmen for improvement of efficiency.

NEED FOR MOTIVATION

Motivation is specially required in sales job as the nature of work is different from other kinds of job in an organisation:

1. Motivation helps in building the morale of salesman; it is the driving force of a salesman. The inactiveness and lethargy of a salesman can be overcome by motivation.

2. As the needs of a salesman are of a wide variety which includes social and physiological needs. They feel that being in a sales job their needs cannot be satisfied.

3. An average job is performed by a salesman to remain in the job and he does not perform to his full capacity.

4. A salesman does not have group relationships because he is posted at far off places and does not have contacts with his fellowmen.

5. There are a lot of health problems because of too much travelling and which impacts the salesman in the long run.

6. The salesman is sandwiched between the supervisor and customer. This is because both want the best from the deal.

7. The work of a salesman is monotonous or in other words highly repetitive. This repetition leads to dissatisfaction.

8. A salesman does not have fixed working hours. He needs to work constantly as he faces acute competition from his competitive products.

9. As the salesman is enveloped by the market and traders, he has no family life.

10. As orders are not easily placed by customers when he visits them, therefore, he has to face a lot of obstacles.

STEPS IN MOTIVATION

Objectives: The salesman must determine the objectives of motivation. These objectives may be different for different salesman. However, encouraging the salesman to give his best is the main aim behind motivation.

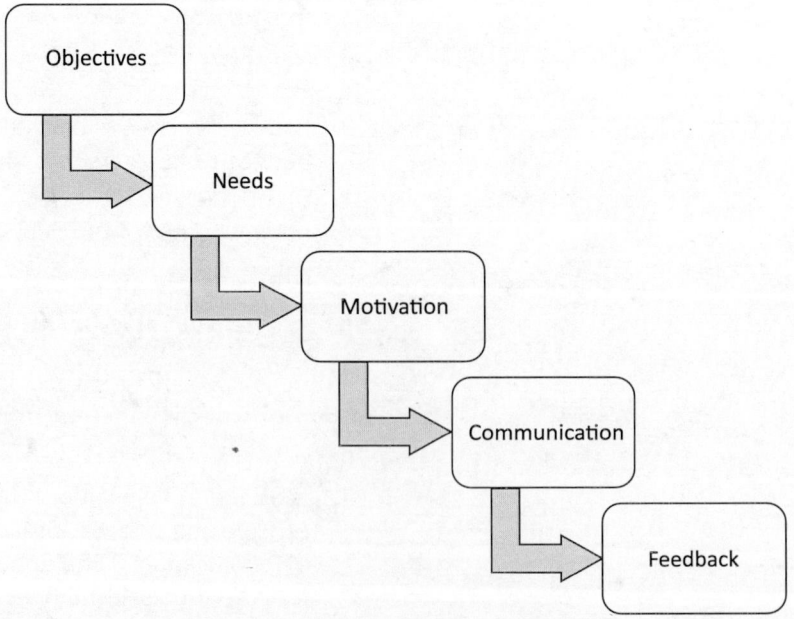

Figure 9.1 Steps in Motivation

Needs: By joining into the depth of expectation of a salesmen, differences between various salesman, positions held by them, their mental attitude; the needs of the salesman can be satisfied.

Motivation of Salesman: Both financial and non-financial incentives can be used to motivate salesmen. By changing the area of work, the salesman can be motivated.

Communication: It is necessary to give special instructions to the salesman, it should be simple and communication should be already understood. For the mutual benefit of both the salesman and the company communication is required.

Feedback: For assessing the effectiveness of the motivational programme it is required to evaluate the results achieved from the motivation programme. For the success of the programme, it is required to develop satisfaction from work and keep development spirit in mind.

MOTIVATIONAL THEORIES

For many years' motivation has been researched by psychologists. There are a number of theories like Likert, Vroom, Herzberg and Maslow which are important and have been discussed in the following paragraphs:

Maslow's Hierarchy of Needs: Abraham Maslow gave this theory where he studied the different types of individual needs. There are five fundamental needs that are required to be studied under Maslow's Hierarchy of Needs.

1. *Physiological Needs:* This is the basic need for survival, for example, hunger, thirst etc.

2. *Safety Needs:* Protection from unpredictable happenings in life like ill health and accidents. As salespeople are fearful whether they would be able to provide minimum level of income for the sustenance of their family.

3. *Belongingness Needs:* Striving to be loved and accepted by those to whom one is close.

4. *Esteem Needs:* Desire for a high reputation and a desire for prestige. A salesperson wants to be more than just a member of the team and needs recognition from team members.

5. *Self-actualization:* The desire for self-fulfilment by achieving what one is capable of achieving.

The theory has great relevance for motivating salesforce even if it states that only after fulfilling lower needs one can look for higher level of needs for motivation. For example, if the physiological needs of a salesperson are not satisfied then the sales manager must offer a suitable income. This theory also states that a satisfied need is not a motivator for the behaviour. To fulfil the social needs, the sales manager must arrange social functions. Secondly, the theory implies that what may be effective with one sales person may not be effective for another. For satisfying the esteem needs sales manager may provide appreciation letters, public recognition and promotions. The self-actualization needs rarely get identified so in such cases mentoring the salespersons is the responsibility of the sales manager.

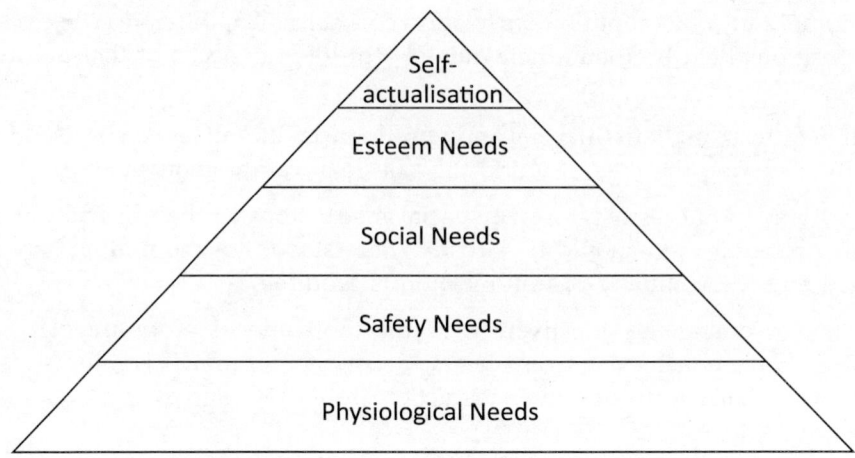

Figure 9.2 Maslow's Hierarchy of Needs

Likert's Sales Management Theory: Likert based his theories on research in contrast to Vroom, Maslow and Herzberg who developed general theories. According to his research the different styles of supervision and salesman's characteristics are related to performance. One of his hypotheses stated that the behaviour of the manager impacts the behaviour of the salesperson. It was found that the sales managers who had high performance goals generally had high performing sales teams. He also compared two methods of sales meetings which included monopolist and group methods. Sales managers who monopolised meetings usually lectured rather than stimulating discussion. On the other hand, sales managers who initiated discussions for sales problems had a tendency of sales teams with higher production.

Vroom's Expectancy Theory: Based on the expectations of a person for success, his motivation to exert effort can be assessed. There are three concepts based on which a person is motivated.

1. *Expectancy:* The perceived relationship of a person between performance and effort which includes higher performance based on increased effort. For example, efforts of a salesperson would include sales calls and long working hours. It would result in increase in new customers, higher level of customer satisfaction and increase in sales.

2. *Instrumentality:* This is based on the relationship between reward and performance. It reflects the extent to which there is a belief that promotion will be awarded on the basis of higher performance. Increase in salary, promotion and recognition are the rewards for a salesperson.

3. *Valence:* The value placed upon a particular reward is represented by the valence. The value of promotion may be high for some individuals and it may be little for others.

For example, a salesperson may believe that by working hard he will achieve increased sales and by high sales it will lead to greater commission and the commission holds high value then it will lead to motivation.

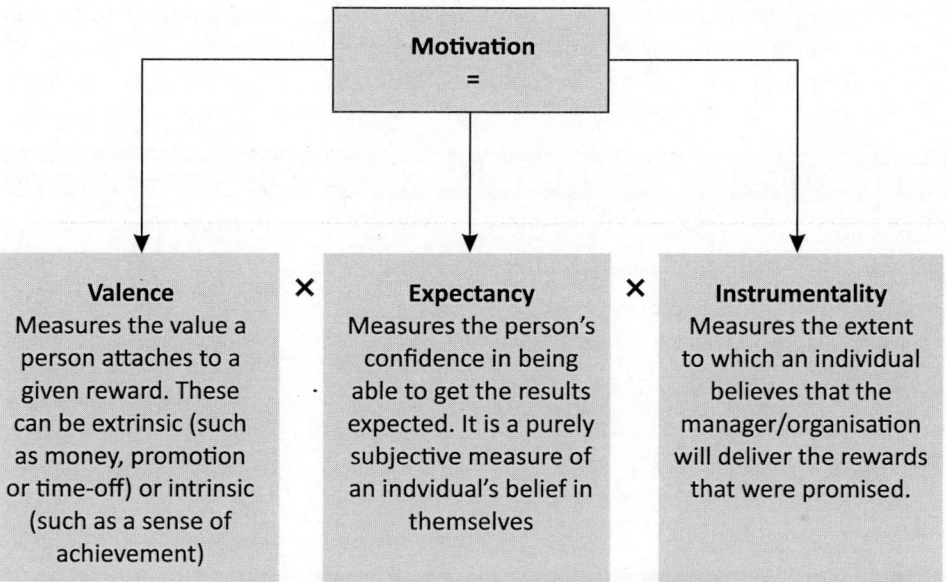

Figure 9.3 Vroom's Expectancy Theory

Herzberg's Theory: The theory given by Herzberg states two distinguishing factors which include hygiene factors that cannot motivate and motivational factors which cause positive motivation. The hygiene factors include interpersonal relationships, salary, security and physical working conditions. The motivational factors included interest value, responsibility exercised by each person, recognition of achievement and concrete achievement. Hygiene factors generally prevent dissatisfaction as their presence is like the physical hygiene of a salesperson. They do not provide any growth in the output of the workers. Thus, they are also known as maintenance factors. On the other hand, motivators are those factors which lead to increase in performance and positively impact job satisfaction of salespersons. Thus, they are also known as satisfiers and are correlated with achievement, growth and recognition.

As higher sales are a motivational factor so a salesperson's achievement is directly observable. Higher responsibility may be provided to salespersons to offer discounts, schedule sales calls and prepare route plans. Such actions provide motivation leading to higher sales success.

The Churchill, Ford, and Walker Model of Salesforce Motivation

This model incorporates a portion of the thoughts of Herzberg and Vroom, which recommends that: The higher the salesman's inspiration, the more noteworthy the work, prompting better execution. This upgraded presentation will prompt more noteworthy prizes which will bring higher work fulfillment. The circle will be finished by the improved fulfillment causing still higher inspiration. The ramifications of this model for team leads are as follows:1. They ought to persuade salesmen that they will sell more by working harder or by being prepared to work 'more intelligent'. 2. They ought to persuade sales reps that the awards for better execution merit the additional work. However, on setting the rewards arbitrarily, the linkage between rewards and performance are weakened.

FINANCIAL MOTIVATION TECHNIQUE

Generally, sales teams prefer financial benefits because they have lower-level needs as compared to self-esteem and self-actualization needs. The financial incentives include:

1. Travelling allowance
2. Profit-sharing
3. Monetary incentives
4. More commission
5. Higher salary
6. Bonus

SELECTING NON-FINANCIAL MOTIVATION TECHNIQUE

The financial benefits have become a poor motivator over the years and companies need to include non-financial incentives to motivate a salesperson. Some of the non-financial motivators include:

1. **Meeting between Salesforce and Manager:** To understand the problems, needs and personality of salesperson. The causes of frustration in salesperson can be better understood through meetings. Further confidence can be boosted and sales technique can be improved.

2. **Job Clarity:** When the expectations from a salesperson and his role in the job is clearly stated then it is a great motivator. The objectives when well defined and duly quantified and linked with recognition and reward serve as a source of motivation for the sales person.

3. **Sales Quotas:** If a sales quota or target is to be effective in motivating a sales person, it must be assumed as attainable and fair. It is sensible to involve a salesperson to participate in the setting of the quota because then he would consider the quota as fair.

4. **Sales Contests:** It is another tool for motivating the sales persons. The purpose of the sales contest is wide. It may encourage the generation of new customers and increase the sales of new products.

5. **Sales Conventions:** It provides the ability to express views, gain social satisfaction and provide opportunities to salespersons for participation. They promote sales person's morale, dissolve social barriers and promote team work.

6. **Positive Effect:** The performance can be up to capabilities in case there is an understanding, human warmth, positive feedback and praise.

7. **Manager's Leadership Style:** Influence through referent power is part of inspirational leadership. In the motivational strategy of the management where identification of charismatic charm is important.

8. **Work Freedom:** The salesperson must be given reasonable freedom and discretion in performing his duties and responsibilities.

9. **Reward and Recognition:** There are more enduring and relatively economic methods of motivation of sales persons' accomplishments.

10. **Persuasion:** Rational methods of persuasion are used for inducing high levels of motivation.

FINANCIAL INCENTIVES

Even though financial incentives are considered a great motivator, still the level of hierarchy at which the salesperson is placed influences his motivation. A financial plan that is administered or developed poorly impacts the trade unions and forces them to go against the management.

CASE STUDY

Spencer corporation, which manufactures calculating machines, with offices in Chennai, Kolkata, Mumbai and Delhi had a large number of sales. It was a small company as compared to others in its competition. The calculating machines sold at a price of ten thousand to forty thousand. Governmental institutes and banks generally use the higher cost machines. These machines offered balancing of columns and rows of large tables and separate keyboards, memory and storage for calculation.

The company also had its own salesforce, wholesalers of electronic machines and industrial distributors. It had four sales managers looking after all four metropolitans mentioned above. These machines were also popular in Sri Lanka and it was managed by Wahib Bhatt Corporation who booked orders from Sri Lanka as well as asking Spencer Corporation to ship goods to Sri Lanka. 40% commission was earned by Wahib Bhatt Corporation on the sales made. However, in reality when the goods were shipped, the commission provided was only 10%. The marketing manager was not satisfied with the sales. The marketing agency could not receive the support of the agents as they were busy in domestic areas. Therefore, the marketing manager made an in-depth study to cite the reasons for the low level of sales. So, he came to know that there was a subsidiary plan for repairing the machines as well. These machines were repaired at a lower cost but were in greater demand. The agents wanted that advertising expenses should be shared with Sri Lanka. They wanted that in place of contractual agreements there should be a long-term agreement with the company.

Questions

1. What should be done by Spencer Corporation to motivate agents?
2. What is the main problem in this situation and how can it be solved?

SUMMARY

There are several ways of defining motivation like "the psychological aspect which helps the salesman to a goal directed behaviour". Motivation is specially required in sales job as the nature of work is different from other kinds of job in an organisation.For many years motivation has been researched by psychologists. There are a number of theories like Likert, Vroom, Herzberg and Maslow which are important. Generally, sales teams prefer financial benefits because they have lower-level needs as compared to self-esteem and self-actualization needs. The financial benefits have become a poor motivator over the years and companies need to include non-financial incentives to motivate a salesperson.

KEY TERMS

Motivation: Motivation is what explains why people or animals initiate, continue or terminate a certain behavior at a particular time.

Maslow's hierarchy of needs: Maslow's hierarchy of needs is a theory of motivation which states that five categories of human needs dictate an individual's behaviour.

Valence: Valence refers to the emotional orientations people hold with respect to outcomes [rewards].

EXERCISES

9.1 Describe Likert's Sales Management Theory. How does it motivate the sales force?

9.2 How does Maslow's Hierarchy assist in spurring the deals with constraining?

9.3 What is the significance of non-monetary motivators in propelling the salesman?

9.4 Why is inspiration of the deal force more significant than the workers in some other circle of movement?

9.5 Describe the need for motivation of salesperson.

9.6 Explain the process of motivating salespersons.

10

Salesforce Compensation

INTRODUCTION

Financial compensation or pay is given the highest importance among the various elements of motivation. Hence, it acts as an important tool for motivation. Sales compensation plans are usually aids for rather than substitutes for motivating employees. A properly designed, sales compensation plan display the following motivational roles:

1. Provide a mechanism for demonstrating the congruency between attaining company's goal and individual goals.
2. Adjustment of pay levels for performance.
3. Provide a living wage.

REQUIREMENTS OF GOOD SALES COMPENSATION PLAN

Following seven requirements are fulfilled by a compensation plan:

1. Attainment of sales organisation's objectives.
2. It is economical to administer.
3. Adjusting the pay according to changing performance.

4. Ease of understanding for sales personnel.
5. The plan is fair and does not penalise sales personnel for uncontrollable factors.
6. The plan fits with the rest of the motivational programme.
7. A secured income is provided in the form of living wages.

DESIGNING A COMPENSATION PACKAGE

I. Examine Job Descriptions

1. Re-examining the nature of the sales job and revising it when it becomes outdated.
2. Analysing the objectives of the sales department for their effect on the sales person's job.
3. Checking out sales volume objectives whether in rupees, number of dealers and distributors, units of products, translating what is expected of sales personnel individually and as a group.
4. Determining the impact of sales related marketing policies.
5. Consideration of current and proposed advertisement and sales promotional programmes.

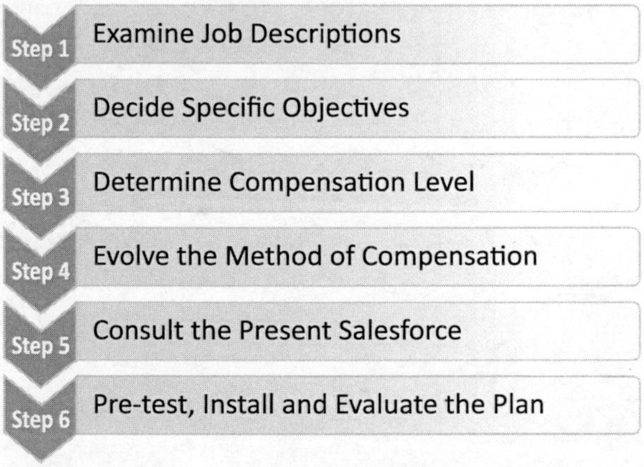

Step 1	Examine Job Descriptions
Step 2	Decide Specific Objectives
Step 3	Determine Compensation Level
Step 4	Evolve the Method of Compensation
Step 5	Consult the Present Salesforce
Step 6	Pre-test, Install and Evaluate the Plan

Figure 10.1 Designing a Compensation Package

II. Decide Specific Objectives

For determining the relative value of individual jobs, it is required to use job evaluation systems. There are four job evaluation methods:

1. **Simple Ranking:** This method of job evaluation is non-expensive. Only overall appraisal of relative worth of jobs is made without attempting to determine critical factors inherent in the job.

2. **Grading:** Various criteria are used for grading the jobs like working conditions, supervision given and received, skills required and job responsibility.

3. **Point System:** This method defines factors commonly associated with the job like education, personality requirements, supervision given and received, responsibility, physical and mental skills.

4. **Factor Comparison Method:** It is similar to the point system but a little complex. To minimise errors, it utilises cross comparisons and scheme of ranking.

Consideration of prevailing compensation patterns in the community is important because compensation patterns are based on external demand and supply factors. Answer to following questions are required:

1. What are the pros and cons of departing from community or industry pattern?
2. What is being done regarding the plans by other companies?
3. For similar positions what is the average compensation plan?
4. What are the compensation systems being used?

III. Determine Compensation Level

On an average the compensation to be received by a salesperson must be determined by the management. An arbitrary judgement basis or individual bargaining may be used to determine the level of compensation.

IV. Evolve the Method of Compensation

There are four basic elements in a compensation plan:

1. Fixed element which provides stability of income in the form of a drawing account or salary.
2. A variable element which serves as an incentive in the form of profit sharing, bonus or commission.
3. An element covering fringe variables like accident benefits, sickness benefits, paid vacations.
4. An element which provides payment of allowances or reimbursement of expenses.

The plan may be constructed in a way that increases the marketing effectiveness. When a salesperson neglects more profitable products and emphasises more on low margin items then the company's earnings are depressed. At times like these selling of better-balanced orders might help in stimulating the compensation plan.

V. Consult the Present Salesforce

Most of the grievances have their root in the compensation plan so management should regularly consult the present sales personnel. Changes required, if any, must be suggested by the sales personnel by articulating the sales personnel to express their likes and dislikes. Suggestions and criticism are appraised relative to the plan or plans under consideration.

VI. Pre-test, Install and Evaluate the Plan

The plan is usually written so that inconsistencies can be eliminated and clarified. After this, the plan is pre-tested. Based on the differences between the current plan that is being used, the amount of testing to be done is decided. For periods representing average, good and poor business speculations can be made in case there is considerable fluctuation in sales pattern.

To eliminate deficiencies or trouble spots there is need to revise the plan. The revised plan undergoes further pre-test when alterations are extensive. However, further testing is not necessary when changes are very minor.

The new plan is explained to the personnel at the time of implementation. The logic and fairness of the plan must be convinced by the management. Explanation is required for changing the plans from the old plan and also their significance.

TYPES OF COMPENSATION PLANS

Straight Salary Plan

This is the simplest plan. The total payment for services is received at regular intervals in the form of fixed sum. This method was used by around 17.5% organisations only. As compared to consumer goods companies it is more common for industrial goods companies.

Advantages

1. Income stability is available.
2. Its administration is economical and simple.
3. Adjusting the work provided is flexible.
4. The sales personnel can be easily directed and controlled.

Disadvantages

1. It affects the morale of the salesperson.
2. There is a rise in the turnover rates when this exists for long.
3. Adjustment with changing circumstances is difficult.

Straight Commission Plan

In this method productivity is the criteria for payment. As sales volume rises to different levels, this method provides regressive and progressive changes in commission rates. This method is broadly classified into two—In first methods the salespeople pay their own expenses. On the other hand, in the second method, the expenses are paid by the company.

Advantages

1. The monetary incentives are mostly provided through this method.
2. Cost control methods are provided.
3. Greater flexibility is provided for revision of commission rates.

Disadvantages

1. Following up of leads is neglected by sales persons.
2. High margin items are neglected and easy to sell, low margin items are pushed.

Salary Plus Commission

Majority of the compensation plans include a combination of commission and salary. These plans tend to add advantages of both, and also, offset disadvantages of both.

Advantages

1. Security of financial incentive as well as income stability.
2. Motivation of the salesforce is greater due to management control.

Disadvantages

1. There are higher clerical costs.
2. The ratio between fixed and variable components varies from 60 : 40 to 80 : 20.

FACTORS INFLUENCING DESIGN OF COMPENSATION SCHEME

While designing the compensation plan of a company, the following factors need to be kept in mind:

Relation with Product Life Cycle

The selling effort is related to the Product Life Cycle as a product moves through the various stages which include introduction, growth, maturity and decline.

Introduction Stage

It is most difficult to sell a product when it is in the introductory stage. In order to establish the product, the salesforce must be willing to travel, enterprising and dynamic. The salesforce must have endurance to pursue the goals, good communication skills and good knowledge of product.

Growth Stage

Maintenance of motivation is a must at this stage. Introduction of indirect incentive schemes is must. For achieving targeted quarters incentives must be linked with them. This will be helpful in the growth of the product.

Maturity Stage

The sales force needs a break after the establishment of the product. In this stage, a basic increase in salary is done, promotions, foreign trips and training programmes in good locations are provided. This is helpful in increasing the knowledge.

Decline Stage

To generate fresh interest in the product that is in the declining stage it is required to provide added incentives. For increasing the sales of the declining product, the product managers who are efficient are given added incentives.

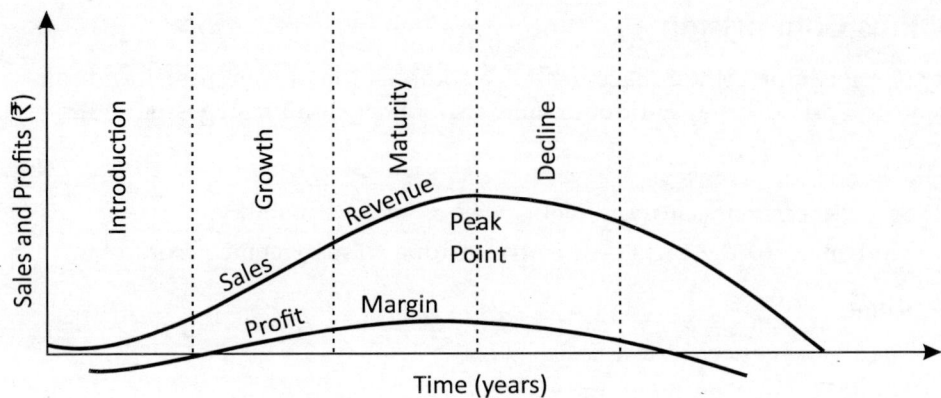

Figure 10.2   Product Life Cycle

Compensation Related with Demographic Characteristics

Based on the demographic characteristics like family life cycle and age; different salespeople prefer different compensation packages. High rewards are promised to those taking high risks but this can mostly be demonstrated by bachelors. Such person can work on a straight incentive or straight commission scheme only. A married person prefers more stability in life.

Role of Selling in the Marketing Strategy of the Company

This refers to how much importance is being given to sales in the marketing mix of a company. This is mainly dependent on the existing competition. The competition may be oligopolistic, monopolistic, pure or no competition.

USE OF BONUS

A bonus is "amount paid for accomplishing a specific sales task". Bonuses are usually paid for carrying out extra assigned tasks, setting up displays, following up leads, obtaining new accounts, performing promotion activities and reaching a sales quota. Bonuses are rarely used alone; they mostly appear along with a main sales compensation plan. For example,

- ◆ When used with straight salary, it resembles the combination plan.
- ◆ When used with straight commission, it includes result to which managerial direction and control are added.
- ◆ When used with salary and commission plans, the bonus becomes a portion of incentive income.

FRINGE BENEFITS

These benefits are not directly related to job performance, ranging from 25–40% of sales compensation packages. These are not high motivation factors as they are part of safety and security needs in Maslow's hierarchy which are lower-level needs. Some companies use "cafeteria approach" for providing fringe benefits wherein the employees can choose from benefits being provided which suit their needs. These are dealt as under:

(i) **Company Benefits:** It composes 25–40% of the basic pay. Company benefits include educational assistance, retirement plans, paid leaves, paid vacation and insurance.

(ii) **Insurance:** These include disability insurance, accident, health insurance and life insurance. Other popular benefits include vision and dental care.

(iii) **Paid Vacation:** Those employees who have served a company for a long time are provided such benefits.

(iv) **Paid Leaves:** Those who have worked in a company for a considerable period of time are given maternity leave and sick leave.

(v) **Retirement Plans:** Many companies provide pension plans for its employees. Through payroll deductions a part of their income is contributed.

(vi) **Educational Assistance:** Company sponsored educational programmes are provided to sales persons. Release time is granted to employees for attending the courses.

(vii) **Salesforce Benefits:** Club membership and company cars are provided for use by employees.

CASE STUDY

The way working trend has changed with the onset of the pandemic, people just didn't look at the salary and days off but looked forward to a work-life balance and thoughtful benefits after pandemic. On the other hand, employers have been given the task of ensuring the well-being of their employees along with excelling in their work environment. The unique needs of employees could be taken into account by massive restructuring.

Salesforce, a cloud-based software company, has kept employee wellbeing as their top priority. They have taken initiatives such as:

Wellness reimbursement program. Through this program, employees are provided acupuncture, nutrition counselling and fitness classes with a reimbursable amount each month.

Parental leave. In this scheme, the primary caregiver is provided 6 months of leave and secondary caregivers with three months leave. This scheme applies to surrogate and adoptive families as well.

Baby bonus. At the time of birth of child or adoption of child, the company provides a baby bonus.

Other programs. B-well together and Thriving mind series focus on strengthening emotional and psychological health by using practical tools such as resources and tips for practicing mindfulness, sleeping well as well as eating right.

Certain teams within the company have also used other programs also like "Wellness days off" i.e. one Friday every month, "Async week" i.e. one week without any meetings and "No-meetings Fridays". The company also offers three ways of working based on the feedback of the employees which includes office based, home based and office flexible flex team agreements. This provides flexibility to the teams in their work like best way of documenting projects and processes, collaboration and communication as well as holding team meetings.

Questions
1. Are the pay and perks provided by Salesforce post-pandemic justified?
2. What are the major benefits provided by Salesforce to ensure the well-being of its employees?
3. Do such benefits complement the productivity of the salesforce?

SUMMARY

Sales compensation plans are usually aids for rather than substitutes for motivating employees. When properly designed, a sales compensation plan has following motivational roles. There are ten steps in designing a compensation plan—Defining a Sales Job, Consider the Company's General Compensation Structure, Consider the Compensation Patterns in Community, Determining Compensation Level, Provide for the Various Compensation Elements, Special Company Needs and Problems, Consult the Present Sales Force, Reduce Tentative Plan to Writing and Pre-test it, Revise the Plan and Implement the Plan and Provide for Follow up. There are three types of compensation plans—Straight Salary Plan, Straight Commission Plan and Salary plus Commission.

KEY TERMS

Compensation: Financial compensation refers to the act of providing a person with money or other things of economic value in exchange for their goods, labour, or to provide for the costs of injuries that they have incurred.

Commission: A sales commission is the amount of compensation paid to a person based on the number of sales generated.

EXERCISES

10.1 Describe the importance of fringe benefits elements with reference to any organisation.

10.2 What is the importance of fringe benefits?

10.3 What are the various types of compensation plans, mention their advantages and disadvantages?

10.4 Describe the requirements of a good compensation plan.

10.5 What are the main elements of a compensation programme?

11

Controlling the Salesforce

LEARNING OBJECTIVES

LO1: To discuss marketing and sales audits for evaluation of a sales organisation's effectiveness

LO2: To carry out sales, marketing cost, profitability and productivity analysis for evaluating the effectiveness of a sales organisation

LO3: To examine purpose and procedure for evaluation and control of performance of the salespeople

LO4: To know the use of salesforce automation tools for performance evaluation and social media as a selling vehicle

INTRODUCTION

Usually, a company's marketing and sales head thinks of various ways for evaluating salespeople and the office branches, analysing problems, and taking corrective measures for improving company's performance. To keep costs under control and monitor salesforce performance, a systematic control mechanism through good sales management programme is required. These techniques help in bringing discipline to the implementation processes as well as keeping the costs within the budget. For salesforce control, mainly two concepts are followed—the sales audit and market analysis.

SALES AUDIT

A salesforce audit is also known as sales management audit which is a prescriptive, diagnostic, systematic and comprehensive tool. The purpose of salesforce audit is "to assess whether a firm's sales management process is adequate, to give direction for performance improvement and to recommend the required changes".

The Evaluation Process of a Salesforce Audit

It is the responsibility of the company's management for finding out the following:

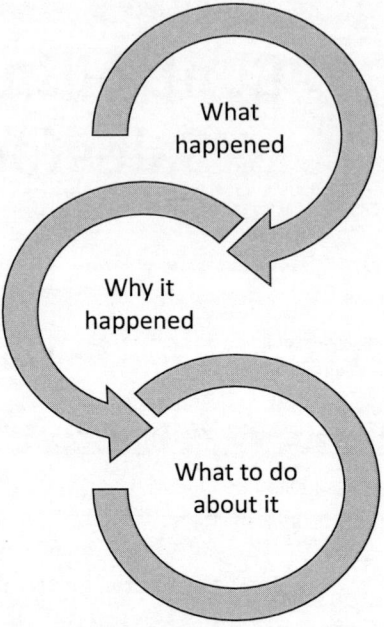

Figure 11.1 Evaluation Process

1. **What happened:** The company should get information by comparing targets with the actual performance. Unfavourable or favourable variations.

2. **Why it happened:** This is a more time consuming and difficult task. The negative variance is affected by what specific factors. These factors include sales managers, salespeople and marketing mix elements.

3. **What to do about it:** This stage consists of leveraging the favourable conditions, overcoming the harmful conditions and corrective actions for solving the problem. For example, if the customer service is not as per customer expectations, first find what kind of service requires improvement pre-sales, during sales and post-sales for taking suitable corrective actions.

EVALUATION OF EFFECTIVENESS OF SALES ORGANISATION

There are several objectives and goals of a sales organisation. Four factors or analysis that are usually required for developing a comprehensive model for evaluating a sales organisation.

Sales Analysis

It is described as "a detailed inspection of a company's sales data, which includes drawing, comparing, classifying and assimilating". The company must decide when a sales is considered complete—whether at the time of paying for the order, shipping it, or receiving it. Majority of the companies complete the sale in its records when an order is transported or shipped.

Framework of Sales Analysis

Three type of decision areas are defined:

1. **All levels in the Sales Organisation:** There are two reasons for which sales analysis is required which includes control and evaluation and identification of problems.

2. **Different Types of Sales:** The sales manager's ability for detecting problems is increased at different organisational levels for different types of sales as shown by analysis.

3. **Different Types of Analysis:** Out of these, interesting information is provided by sales quotas by comparing actual sales.

Sales Report

Sales performance monitoring is done through sales reports. Depending on the product and its movement, a weekly or daily report is submitted. It assists in portfolio planning, cost planning and product planning. The seasonality of sales is revealed through weekly sales report. Whereas quarterly figures are obtained through monthly figures. For example:

1. Contribution in terms of value for each product. Maximisation of this contribution is needed.

2. Sales are broken down on the basis of geographic regions for monitoring sales performance.

3. Whether the salesman is focusing on the right kind of customer can be demonstrated through customer break-up or sales.

Regional Sales Analysis

Through sales analysis the strength of sales in a region is indicated. Based on the population of a region, the sales figure is estimated. Boundaries of the region should be permanent for comparing the trend over a long period of time. In addition to area-wise, product-wise, volume and value categorisation of sales should be made through various types of outlets such as retailers and wholesalers. This can further be classified into super bazaars, departmental stores and cooperatives. A summary of annual, quarterly and monthly reports should be prepared in the form of a formal report.

MARKETING COST ANALYSIS

Marketing cost analysis "analyses sales volume and selling expenses to determine the relative profitability of particular aspects of sales operations". The initial step in marketing cost analysis is sales analysis by marketing channels, size of order, class of account, products, sales personnel and territories. The next step includes breaking down the selling expenses on basis of sales territories.

Marketing Cost Analysis Techniques

Classifying Selling Expenses: Marketing cost analysis needs classification of selling expenses into common (indirect) and separable (direct) expenses. A common expense is "one that is not traceable to specific sales personnel, sales territories, customers, marketing channels and products". A separable expense is "one traceable to individual sales personnel, sales territories, customers, marketing channels and products". Depending on the operation under study and company policies, a given expense may be common or separable.

Converting Accounting Expense Data to Activity Expense Groups: Expenses are recorded according to their immediate purpose based on the conventional accounting system. For instance, bad-debt expense, general and administrative expenses, general selling expense, advertising expense, branch sales office rent, sales travel expense, sales commissions and sales salaries.

Bases for Allocating Common Expenses: It is troublesome for selecting bases for allocation of common expenses. In contrast to analysing the cost of production which requires only the number of machine hours as a single allocation basis, other forms of marketing cost analysis require marketing and selling expenses on several bases. Allocation bases are "factors that measure variability in the activities for which specific expenses are incurred".

Contribution Margin: Contribution margin is defined as follows:

Contribution margin = net sales – cost of goods sold – (separable expenses + common expenses allocable on logical bases)

In other words, it is the "dollar amount to cover unallocated common expenses and profit (if any).

Tools for Control

For the control of channel members, two conventional methods are used which include power and contract.

Contract: In Indian context, the most common and oldest tool for control is contract. Contract can be defined as "an agreement enforceable by law". It may be in example or oral or written. In relatively, long term relationships, the agreement is generally in written format in order to avoid ambiguity and impart clarity. Some of the common elements of contract are as follows:

(a) Payments

(b) Term

(c) Advertising and sales promotion

(d) Prices and margins

(e) Installation and repairs

(f) Inventory

(g) Territory to be covered

(h) Classes of types of customers

(i) Product handled

Power: For controlling the channels of distribution another tool is power. When one member depends on another then it leads to power wherein either one of them or both are able to influence the achievements of another.

Kinds of Control Devices

These are classified into three kinds as follows:

Distribution Audit: Distribution audit is a comprehensive and systematic analysis of all activities and results of a distribution programme. It assumes that appropriate programmes and policies can produce positive results which can be identified, achieved and evaluated by the distributor.

Dealer Relations Index: For the measurement of the entire distribution programme, this quantitative technique is used. In this technique a composite index is prepared taking into account a number of strategic items including sales displays and after sales services.

Reports and Budgets: These are perhaps the most frequently used control devices. An established reporting system brings information on a monthly, daily or weekly basis. Experiences are shared with other dealers in such reports.

Salesforce Evaluation and Control Procedure

1. Setting policies on performance control and evaluation
2. Deciding the bases of salespeople's performance evaluation
3. Establishing performance standards
4. Comparing standards and the actual performance
5. Review performance evaluation with salespersons
6. Decide sales management control and actions

Basic Issues in Salesman's Evaluation

1. Periodicity of evaluation: Very long-term evaluation is not desirable and correct results may not be provided by short-term evaluation.
2. Performance standards should be realistic so that comparison can be made accurately.

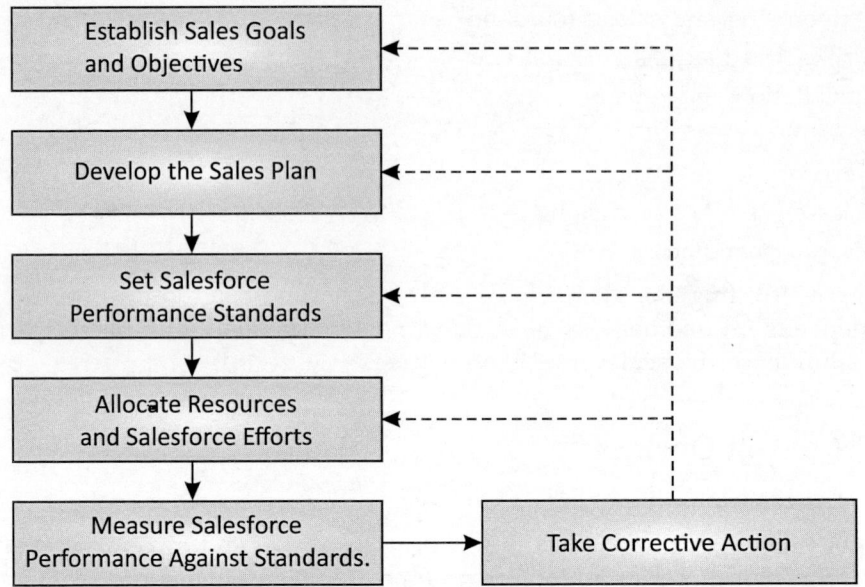

Figure 11.2 A Contemporary Approach to Salesforce Performance Evaluation

3. The database or accounting system of the company. Precise comparison cannot be provided on the basis of data taken from a typical sales record.

4. As conditions differ so comparison cannot be made on a "man to man" basis.

5. The evaluation can be made on quantitative data which can vitiate evaluation results.

SALESFORCE AUTOMATION

Since the beginning of 1990s, salespeople and sales managers have received help from sales force automation. It is defined as "SFA is the application of computerised technologies to support salespeople and sales management in the achievement of their work-related objectives." The ecosystem of SFA includes: service providers, infrastructure and hardware suppliers and SFA solution providers.

Service Providers: They are needed for conducting customer analysis, planning training programmes, changing an organisation structure and selling process. Service providers can help achieve success for SFA projects and also to a large extent contribute to the project.

Hardware and Infrastructure Vendors: Inside sales managers and salespeople use laptop and desktop from suppliers of hardware. Outside or field salespeople often need laptop computers and hand-held devices. Wireless or mobile solutions are needed for the field.

SFA Solutions Providers: SFA solution providers are of different types. SFA specialists concentrate on a particular activity or function. For instance, product configurator is a software-based application engine that allows a company to configure a complex product or service based on pre-defined rules.

SOCIAL MEDIA

Social media refers to Google Plus, LinkedIn, Facebook and Twitter where people can come to communicate with each other irrespective of the location. Use of social media for interacting with prospects until the prospect is ready to buy is called social selling.

Benefits of Social selling

1. **Real Time Communication:** Two-way communication of opinions, views and ideas between company and customers is increased while using social media. For the promotion of products and services, a good opportunity is provided to the companies. For example, a dissatisfied customer may post his problem with social media to which the company may respond by suggesting ways to resolve the problem.

2. **Improved Visibility:** People gather knowledge about a company and its salespersons once a salesperson involves himself on social platforms by sharing his suggestions, ideas and views.

3. **Increased Customer Loyalty and Relationship:** The desire and interest towards buying action is gathered with salesperson's engagement and involvement.

CASE STUDY

Digitex LLC has been growing over the Middle East since 1998. The company distributes electronic equipment and parts in the Gulf Cooperation Council region. Digitex has strict control over procedures and policies over its business environment both externally and internally. However, the business environment is semi-computerised.

Processing customer order: Order from the customers arrive either from field representative, telephone or email. These orders are shipped to customers after the necessary processing. The processing of orders is computerised and drop-down menus are used for selection of bar codes. Prices are selected automatically against each part that is selected.

Business transaction: The company has many customers both new and old. Even though the new customers have been in business for many years, they started to trade with Digitex recently. On the other hand, some other customers had been trading with Digitex for 6–8 years. Most existing customers have payment period between 1–3 months and are given credit facilities. Credit facility provided to new customers is subject to checking of customers according to the company's policy. A hierarchy is followed for approving credit facilities of Digitex customers which ranges from Board of Directors to senior managers.

The policy requires that in order to apply for credit requires the following:

1. Have been in business for at least past seven years with audit accounts as evidence

2. They should provide at least last 5 years bank statements to prove their existence

3. New customers must provide 5 references from existing suppliers with whom they have been trading

4. Existing suppliers must have traded with the new customers for at least 1 year 5. New customers must provide their business cash flow forecast for next three years

Cash Transaction Cycle: Upon receipt of cash from customers the sales cycle gets completed. The records are updated after receiving cash from customers. The company's normal practice is to demand cheque payments, however, sometimes customers send cash directly to Digitex account. The cheques received are handled by a cashier. The cashier may collect cash personally from some of the customers by directly visiting their business.

Question

1. Assess the performance of Digitex based on sales performance evaluation criteria.

SUMMARY

Salesforce audit is "to assess whether a firm's sales management process is adequate, to give direction for performance improvement and to recommend the needed changes". There are several objectives and goals of a sales organisation. Four factors or analysis that are usually required for developing a comprehensive model for evaluating a sales organisation. Sales performance monitoring is done through sales reports. Depending on the product and its movement, a weekly or daily report is submitted. It assists in portfolio planning, cost planning and product planning. For the control of channel members, three conventional methods are used which include structure, power and contract.

KEY TERMS

Sales audit: The Sales Audit is the comprehensive, systematic, periodic, analysis, evaluation and interpretation of business environment, objectives, strategies, principles to determine the areas of problem or opportunities and recommending the plan of action to improve the sales performance.

Sales analysis: A sales analysis is a detailed report that shows a business's sales performance, as well as customer data and generated revenue.

Social selling: Social selling is the practice of using a brand's social media channels to connect with prospects, develop a connection with them and engage with potential leads.

EXERCISES

11.1 How does monitoring help in performance evaluation of salesforce?

11.2 What are the needs of monitoring and describe the parameters used in monitoring a salesforce?

11.3 Discuss the various marketing cost analysis techniques.

11.4 Describe the salesforce automation ecosystem.

11.5 What are the basic issues in salesman's evaluation?

11.6 Discuss the benefits of social selling.

12

Managing International Salesforce

LEARNING OBJECTIVES

LO1: To appreciate the reasons for International Sales

LO2: To understand the challenges faced by international sales manager

LO3: To know the qualities of international sales manager

LO4: To describe the entry strategies for international sales and marketing

LO5: To discuss advanced international selling

LO6: To understand the risks involved in doing international business

INTRODUCTION

International markets vary in terms of their development level. At one end there are highly developed and affluent markets in the Western countries and, on the other end, there are underdeveloped and poor markets such as Africa. Depending on the level of development, there was a difference in types of products sold in each market. Generally, global manufacturers and traders try to outsource products without losing of quality with a definite cost advantage. When companies do not understand selling in international markets then they are unable to take advantage of this opportunity.

REASONS FOR INTERNATIONAL SALES

An important element of marketing is sales. All individuals from different countries need to sell something in order for survival. The selling activities are carried out throughout the world. International sales managers have to guide and coordinate in the efforts of sales organisations where the company does business. An important role in the international market is played by personal selling.

Growth is promised in the international markets in cases when the domestic market has been saturated. Thus, an opportunity for selling is provided by the international market. The life cycle of a product is different in different countries. A single product can be in the introduction stage in one country and any of the other three stages in other countries. Since, globally oriented firms attain upto 50% of the total revenues out of overseas sales, many smaller firms are also attracted to move to international markets.

CHALLENGES FACED BY INTERNATIONAL SALES MANAGER

There are three kinds of challenges which include the following:

Economic: A major role in global sales strategies is played by economic factors. Economic factors in the form of Gross Domestic Product decide the level of purchasing power. Economic development can be classified into following:

1. *Developed Economies:* These include Canada, Japan, US and majority of the western European countries. These countries have high levels of disposable income and dominate the economic system through the private enterprises.

2. *Developing Economies:* These are comparatively at a lower stage of development economically. Economic system in these countries is shifting to domestic development from export-led growth. These include Venezuela, Taiwan and South Korea.

3. *Underdeveloped Economies:* As these countries are in the pre-industrial stage of economic development. Therefore, in these countries the standard of living is low. Example, Haiti, Pakistan, Ethiopia.

Legal: Hurdles in International Sales are created by legal constraints and trade barriers posed by the government. Very high duty for imports is imposed by certain governments. For example, on importing cars, a duty of 300% is charged in Columbia. Other nations like Japan impose restrictions on products like telecommunications equipment, agricultural commodities, and medical equipment. Some countries have imposed a total ban on import-export because of political differences like India-Pakistan, US-Cuba. Many third world countries like the Middle East and Saudi Arabia only permit partnership with local companies and do not allow total ownership.

Cultural: The distinctive way of life of people comes under culture. The pattern of living of a group of people also comes under this. Many factors are included under the cultural differences like time, space, tastes, food habits, dress, multiplicity of languages, language barrier. There is importance of these factors for sales management and personal selling.

These differences are visible in private and business customs also. Like North Americans approach a business directly, firmly, personally and in a straightforward manner. On the other hand, Latin people like to know the other personally before talking about business. In Japanese culture patience is important as Japanese people ask many questions before the sale takes place.

Body language and hand gestures are essentially required for effective communication. For example, while greeting customers, Europeans and Americans shake hands. On the other hand, a namastey or bow from the waist is given in other countries like Japan and other Asian countries. Eating habits also differ between countries as many countries avoid pork while some totally avoid non-vegetarian food.

Figure 12.1 Namastey in India

QUALITIES OF INTERNATIONAL SALES FORCE

A successful salesman must have following qualities:

Decision Making: Even if limited information is provided, the salesman must be able to take the decisions. In international selling the risks are of much greater dimension. The salesman must not keep the customer waiting for the final decision from the headquarters.

Knowledge: For the correct interpretation of data obtained, the salesperson should have enough knowledge. A part of his duties and tasks is research.

Cultural Adaptability: For developing trust by the buyer, the salesman must develop credibility and he should also develop credibility with the other employees. There are many hurdles which need to be overcome and no supervision is required in the host country. He should be able to show a great amount of responsibility and discharge his duties responsibly.

Physical Fitness*:* In different climates, physical fitness is important as the work of travelling is very demanding and laborious. There is a lot of strain on the salesman regarding food and other details like serving.

Language: He should be skilled in the language appropriate for the host country. The differences in terminology of different countries may be distinguishable, for example, Britain and USA.

British say Cinema	Americans say theatre
British say petrol	Americans say gas
British say bedroom	Americans say living room
British say biscuit	Americans say cookie
British say lift	Americans say elevator
British say flat	Americans say apartment

ENTRY STRATEGIES FOR INTERNATIONAL SALES AND MARKETING

One of the major issues in international marketing is whether the same marketing strategy should be applicable to all countries or it may vary based on the local market. Sometimes there is difference in marketing mix and sales strategies because of technical specifications and local competitive pressures. After determinating of information, the company needs to decide the entry mode into the overseas market. This can be done in the following ways:

Passive Exporting: When orders are received from the overseas market, they are unsolicited and come automatically as the name of the company is listed or shown in trade directories.

Active Exporting: This is done usually by intermediaries and the company's sales force. The company actively participates in exports when the volume of sales increases. Proper feedback is not provided by this method even if it is economical.

Direct Exporting: In this salesperson directly deals with ultimate consumers or intermediaries in the overseas market.

Licencing: Granting usage of contractual permission in distinct property rights such as trademarks, patents in a particular geographic area during a particular time period.

Counter Trade: Use of bartering arrangement at least partially in foreign sales which includes sending goods to foreign countries for exchange of products.

Joint Ventures: This includes foreign partners in participation. The political problems of the firm are reduced in this way. Joint ventures exist commonly in Japan and America.

Wholly-owned Subsidiaries: A parent company owns the overseas units. In developed countries, they are permissible but they require substantial investment.

Management Contracts: When the operations of overseas owners are managed by home countries they are known as management contracts. International chains make use of this commonly like Sheraton and Hilton.

ADVANCED INTERNATIONAL SELLING

There are several important considerations that need to be taken care of during international selling:

1. The salesperson must have effective communication. He should give proper importance to delivery, speed, quality to language and execution. The listener's comprehension is affected by this.

2. Visual aids must be used to a greater extent by the sales person. He should be particularly careful about humour and choose example as illustrations. Due to differences in culture and society, use of jokes and humour is risky in an international setting. When questions are asked, multiple answers or alternative answers should be provided as people are fearful of making errors because of difficulty in language.

3. Special communication challenges are faced by Japanese customers. As compared to Americans, they are more reserved. As Japanese customers are not able to respond to open-ended questions, salesman must try to be polite with them.

4. Different impacts are made by cultural differences. Example, French people hesitate when talking about the price of things or money related matters. However, American people don't feel uncomfortable when talking about money.

5. Plenty of time must be allowed for appointments in Italy. They like to spend a lot of time chatting with the salesperson. Swiss people welcome business cards and have a great deal of respect for titles and degrees. Speaking Portuguese is considered as a matter of pride for Brazilians. Sense of touch is considered as a means of communication in the Arab world.

Due to the saturation in the domestic market, international selling gained importance. For making proper marketing and sales strategies, there is a need to process a lot of information. For successful international selling there is a need to tackle environmental challenges in the best possible manner. For companies that aspire to become global, the mode of entry is also an important requirement. The recruitment, selection and training of salesmen are some of the aspects that require consideration. There are good chances of success in international sales if these aspects are taken care of.

RISKS INVOLVED IN DOING INTERNATIONAL BUSINESS

International business has two main risks:

♦ **Political Risks:** Due to sudden political developments such as wars and coups it involves disruption of payments or contracts. As a consequence of it, businesses expropriated, payments can be withheld or cancelled. There have been situations in which payment has been delayed even after goods are supplied as per contract.

♦ **Commercial and Financial Risks:** Financial risks involve failure of the buyer to pay as per contact due to bankruptcy. Commercial risks involve sudden change in buyer's situation like a sudden change in foreign currency.

CASE STUDY

Hindustan Perfumes Limited, a renowned company in India manufactured two varieties of perfume. One was based on alcohol and the other on essential oils. These were exported to countries in the Middle East. Particularly the essential oil perfumes called "Attars" were focused on orthodox sections of the society. The price of these perfumes was very high ranging from 20,000 to 30,000/kg. The price went higher upto ₹2,00,000/kg. These perfumes were in high demand. The other alcohol-based perfumes were mostly available in the form of sprays. Both types of perfumes were concentrated upon by the company. The competition was much fierce among western labels like Chanel, Yardley and English Leather.

The company started its business by booking orders for both types of perfumes through sales representatives. The salesmen were able to procure a few orders but these orders were not followed through by customers. After every few months the company sent its representatives for fresh order booking. A lot of expenses were involved as the process was cumbersome. So, the management thought of appointing local deals for order taking. Another problem was that some of the consignments incurred damages. Sometimes the goods also got spoiled due to late dispatch. No suitable solution was found even when the company tried to negotiate this aspect with the local agents. The company was keen to establish its business in foreign lands and was trying to find a selling strategy that was suitable.

Questions

1. Which method of selling would be recommended by you and the strategy in sales promotion?

2. What could have been the drawback in this approach and knowledge of salesmen for not being successful?

SUMMARY

An important element of marketing is sales. All individuals from different countries need to sell something in order to surve. The selling activities are carried out throughout the world. International sales managers have to guide and coordinate in the efforts of sales organisations where the company does business. There are three kinds of challenges which include the following—Economic, legal and cultural. For the success of a salesman many qualities are required. One of the major issues in international marketing is whether the same kind of marketing must be followed for all countries or different according to local market. Sometimes due to differences in marketing mix and sales strategies because of technical specifications and local competitive pressures. There are several important considerations that need to be taken care of during international selling. Due to the saturation in the domestic market, international selling gained importance. For making proper marketing and sales strategies, there is a need to process a lot of information. For successful international selling there is a need to tackle environmental challenges in the best possible manner.

KEY TERMS

International sales: International Sales means sales outside of the territory of the country.

Exporting: Exporting is defined as the sale of products and services in foreign countries that are sourced or made in the home country.

Licensing: Licensing is defined as the granting of permission by the licenser to the licensee to use intellectual property rights, such as trademarks, patents, brand names, or technology, under defined conditions.

Joint venture: A joint venture is a combination of two or more parties that seek the development of a single enterprise or project for profit, sharing the risks associated with its development.

EXERCISES

12.1 What are the modes of entery into the overseas market and what considerations affect international sales?

12.2 What qualities must be possessed by the salesman engaged in international sales?

12.3 What factors must be considered by salesmen engaged in international sales?

12.4 How does international sales management differ from domestic sales management?

13

Managing Sales During Crisis

LEARNING OBJECTIVES

LO1: To describe the various types of crises

LO2: To discuss the response to crisis

LO3: To understand the key to handling the response to crisis

LO4: To redefining sales management during crisis

INTRODUCTION

It is not always that the sales team faces normal situations. There are many instances when the situation goes out of hand. In such situations, the sales team cannot function normally. In order to recover from crises, it is important to implement sales efforts effectively. Some of common types of crises are discussed below.

TYPES OF CRISIS

1. **Falling through a Huge Deal:** Having a resilient sales process helps in allocating resources, predicting revenue and forecasting sales. However, such a process is not flawless and sometimes the deals may turn unsuccessful. Prospects may go through changes that forbid them from purchasing the product.

2. **Churning of a Massive Client:** A massive churn means that there exists a gap in the forecasted revenue which has a potentially massive impact on the whole company. Not only this, in order to make up for the lost revenue,

there is a lot of pressure on the entire sales team on losing a recurring stream of revenue.

3. **Resignation, Dismissal or Illness of a Key Member:** This can occur due to personal reasons like illness or job-related reasons like dismissal or resignation. When a team member leaves for job in another company, the other team members bear the burden of his work. Moreover, the other team members may question their future with the company.

4. **Slashing of Funding:** The morale of a team topples down when there are budget cuts. Sales and training collateral might be impacted besides the impact on travel and hiring costs. There may be a lot of trouble when the training budget is taken away after expectations are set based on a well-trained team.

5. **Missing a Series of Targets:** There is optimism in the best salespersons, but optimism is not enough for convincing superiors when significant targets are missed. Every day the sales team has the challenge of dealing with pushbacks and objections. A lot of unforeseeable circumstances and uncertain situations need to be dealt with. When things do not go as planned, the salesperson has to take responsibility and deal with the associated anxiety.

6. **Occurrence of a Disciplinary Issue:** Any kind of misconduct may occur at the workplace, say, from insubordination and poor time management to serious matters like illegal activities. When a disciplinary issue occurs, it takes an emotional toll on the entire sales team including the person involved.

Figure 13.1 Covid-19

7. **Global Crisis:** Crisis is mostly out of control, as in case of Covid-19 there was a far-reaching impact which left everyone powerless. All the above-mentioned crises can occur within a global crises that has both financial and health implications. Even if it seems difficult to deal with a global crisis, still one can prepare for its business-related impacts by planning in advance at each step.

RESPONSE TO CRISIS

1. **Being Transparent:** When a crisis hits a sales team, the facts should not be hidden from the team members. The team should not be deceived and they should be made aware of the reality. On the other hand, the situation should also not be exaggerated that it may create panic. Everyone just needs to be transparent. Even if one feels that the information needs to be kept secret but then also it is best when everyone stays informed.

2. **Seeking Ideas from Team Members:** In order to make everyone able to deal with crises, it is important to empower the employees so that they may contribute in giving solutions. Every member is unique in a sales team. These members were hired because of their skills, qualities and traits. Every member has a unique set of experiences from his/her previous role. Highly engaged employees tend to provide high return on investment and also higher performance.

3. **Empathising with the Team:** During crises it is generally the impulse of sales manager to just give orders. However, he must not do so and must empathise with the team by hearing their problems. The employees' problems must be dealt with honesty as it is the moral obligation of a sales manager to acknowledge their emotions and thoughts.

4. **Focusing on What can be Controlled:** The team members must not be forced to pursue a deal as sometimes the prospect may be unqualified. In case of missed targets, churned customers and failed deals; the pressure must not be put on the team. When a companywide crisis is going on, it is better to work on things that can be controlled.

5. **Addressing the Problem at Hand:** After the crises has occurred, the changes that led to it might be long term or permanent. So, at first it is required to look back and assess whatever has happened. Whether it is related to the cut in budgets or dismissal of an employee, no problem should be left without an answer. Secondly, since the team members went through an emotional turmoil, it is the duty of the sales manager to thank them for patiently dealing with it. Finally, if any member went out of his way in dealing with the situation, then his role must be appreciated.

6. **Refocusing on the Company Values, Projects and Goals:** Generally, a sales crisis leaves the sales team exhausted and drained. Their motivation levels are lowered and they need some time before everything returns back to normal.

For increasing the energy levels, it is required to:

♦ Celebrate small as well as big wins as a team.

♦ Check-ins in the morning and afternoon to find out progress and rough parts in the day.

♦ Allowing time for resting and recharging.

Ultimately, providing the team with support, training and feedback is of utmost importance for reinforcing the hard work of employees.

KEY TO HANDLING SALES CRISIS

Crises are generally stressful to people whom they impact. Best way to handle a crisis is to deal with things that can be impacted and letting go of things that cannot be dealt with. Open communication with the sales team is of utmost importance otherwise the stress would spill to all team members. When a crisis occurs, following things need to be kept in mind:

♦ Organising direct meeting with sales representatives and providing full support to team members.

♦ Doing the best of what one can by reinforcing the skills and strengthening the team's pipelines.

♦ Setting new goals, refreshing the team's energy and taking time to recap the situation.

A crisis can be handled by allowing the team to be empowered. By being open and honest with the team creates better connection and helps them tackle whatever comes their way.

REDEFINING SALES MANAGEMENT DURING CRISIS

Covid pandemic has highlighted how a traditional sales team with target of hitting particular sales is different from a purpose-driven sales team developed for the cause of improving customer's lives.

When teams sell with noble purpose, trust and graciousness which enables them to be:

♦ **Revenue-generating:** Main focus is improvement in the customer's life.

♦ **Resilient:** In the case of adversity only those can survive who have belief in a bigger cause.

♦ **Relevant:** On the basis of value and impact they build deep relationships.

Redefining sales in a Covid-impacted World

The Covid-19 has transformed the buyer seller-relationship due to the shift to video sales calls and remote working. The traditional approach of "sell, sell, sell" is quite pushing and rather than engaging customer it is likely to be off-putting. For avoiding such problems, sales leaders need to point their teams towards a higher purpose than money in order to drive the revenue.

Selling Noble Purpose, Trust and Graciousness

Little value is provided by quota-focused traditional approach as viewed from the eyes of the customer. The sales team needs to focus more on the customers. More specific shift in mindset is required for providing more relevance. Selling with a noble purpose does not only mean pleasing the customers, it deals with alignment of entire organisation towards improvement in customer's condition.

How to Inspire Sales Teams to Jump-start with a Sense of Urgency

1. **Aligning Sales Team around Clear Customer Impact:** This means allowing customers to focus more on their families by saving their time. Allowing better leveraging of data by customers for making informed decisions. Increasing the profitability of customers, investing for growth and keeping the business running.

2. **Shifting the Sales Ecosystem towards Customers:** Behaviours and beliefs are shaped according to the messages, processes and systems. Leaders must shift the traditional sales ecosystem to create compelling sales teams. Leaders must understand how sales presentations are structured, the type of customer intelligence salespeople capture, how meetings are run, what gets rewarded and CRM system tracks.

3. **Building Trusted Relationships by Reframing Customer Interactions:** The virtual Covid-19 environment has made people more practical and direct by stripping away the niceties and revealing the intent more clearly. Customers generally do not feel happy about sitting through self-serving discovery calls and product presentations.

Creating a "From/To" Shift Transforms the Sales Process

The entire sales process is transformed when leaders commit to selling with a noble purpose. It is ironic that a sales team makes more money even when it has a higher purpose than making money.

The Freedom to Make Money and Make a Difference

Selling with noble purpose, trust and graciousness requires more emotional intelligence and strategic discipline and it yields sales teams, customers and everyone alike.

CASE STUDY

Unieuro is a large consumer electronics retailer that used to sell offline before the pandemic. During the pandemic the store had to avoid crowding and could be opened only for limited number of hours. Still there was fear among the consumers regarding infection. As a result of this, online sales rose for majority of the retailers. In case of Unieuro, the balance got shifted from 90% offline and 10% online to 50%–50%. In order to manage online orders, several employees were shifted.

The main focus of the study is around the time of the first lockdown. As Unieuro was able to successfully manage the Pandemic and shift quickly online, it had become difficult to maintain the 50–50 balance. Thus, the following two situations persisted which needed to be considered:

First, decreasing share of online sales by forfeiting gains made during the pandemic by leveraging on the offline sales, where Unieuro is strong in customer assistance and up-selling.

Second, to increase the online sales, leveraging on the better customer information provided by the analytics, on the growing trend of e-commerce and lower managing costs of the website.

What is of interest is the fact that none of the situations is a win-win because both channels have mixed advantages and disadvantages and seem to be targeting different customer segments. This was shown by the performance metrics of Unieuro online and reports on the perception of customers.

Questions

1. In what way can a correct balance be defined between online and offline sales?
2. Whether a leading or ancillary role should be given to the offline stores.
3. Describe the difference in shopping experience offered by offline and online stores.
4. Is the crisis management strategy adopted by Unieuro justified?

SUMMARY

Managing sales during crises requires firstly an understanding of the various types of crises. Crises are generally stressful to people whom they impact. Best way to handle a crisis is to deal with things that can be impacted and letting go of things that cannot be dealt with. Open communication with the sales team is of utmost importance otherwise the stress would spill to all team members. Covid pandemic has highlighted how a traditional sales team with target of hitting particular sales is different from a purpose-driven sales team developed for the cause of improving customer's lives.

KEY TERM

Crisis: A time of great danger or difficulty; the moment when things change and either improve or get worse.

EXERCISES

13.1 Discuss the various types of crises faced by a sales team.

13.2 What are the different ways of responding to a crisis?

13.3 How can the sales crisis be handled?

13.4 How can sales management be redefined during a crisis?

SECTION 2
DISTRIBUTION MANAGEMENT

14

Distribution Management
An Introduction

INTRODUCTION

Distribution channels are required because most of the customers cannot be reached directly by the companies. The members of the distribution channels include retailers, wholesalers, agents, stockists, dealers, distributors, carrying and selling agents (C&SAs) and carrying and forwarding agents (C&FAs). Depending on the markets and the product that they service, a set of channel members are used by companies which is a combination of direct company distribution. Distribution channels provide the right situation for possession, place and time utilities for the company.

DEFINITION OF DISTRIBUTION MANAGEMENT

Havaldar and Cavale define it as follows:

♦ The management of all activities which facilitates movement and coordination of supply and demand in the creation of time and place utility in goods.

♦ The art and science of determining requirements, acquiring them, distributing them and finally maintaining them in an operationally ready condition for their entire lives.

♦ Broad range of activities concerned with the efficient movement of finished products from the end of the production line to the consumer and, in some cases, it also includes the movement of raw materials from the source of supply to the beginning of the production line.

Companies generally believe that distribution can best be performed by themselves and usually they undertake distribution related activities. For this purpose, building and maintaining a large workforce was mandatory. With the rise in population direct selling to customers became unmanageable. Hence, they started looking for people who could do this job better, i.e., intermediaries.

As the name implies, intermediaries are the link between customers and manufacturers. Their primary job is to provide the product to the customer which they do by re-distributing the products manufactured by the company.

NEED FOR DISTRIBUTION CHANNELS

Generally, the following functions are performed by intermediaries or channel members:

♦ Accumulation, aggregation and sorting of the right kind of goods for meeting consumer needs at the purchase point.

♦ Believing in routine and simplified transactions and working with a huge number of products for the minimisation of distribution costs.

♦ To help manage the business better by providing information both to buyers and sellers.

♦ To buy vast variety of goods by comparing costs for making appropriate recommendations to customers.

♦ To be aware of the environment in which they operate and hence isolate the companies from direct impact of the local conditions.

♦ Reduction in number of touch points. The company will not be able to meet demands of thousands of customers directly and hence needs intermediation.

Are Distribution Channels Necessary

The right answer to this would be sometimes and not always. This is for the following reasons:

♦ With the advent of the Internet, many companies like Dell, Amazon, Snapdeal and Flipkart have grown in plenty as they deal with customers directly.

♦ Bata sells its branded footwear directly to customers through its own outlets.

♦ Eureka Forbes is a well-known company which does not keep physical stocks of its products. It calls the customers and sells products directly at their homes.

OVERVIEW OF DISTRIBUTION CHANNELS

The broad classification of distribution channels is as follows:

- **Sales Channel:** It has the function of financing the transactions, negotiating fair bargains, sharing information between company and consumer as well as motivating buyers
- **Delivery Channel:** It is meant only for physical transactions
- **Service Channel:** They perform after sales services like in Maruti service station

Each channel has some unique characteristics that serve some objectives for the companies in different locations:

Carrying and Forwarding Agents (C&FA)

This category is known as facilitators. Basically, transporters who act as a mid-point between distributors and companies are the C&FAs. The C&FAs do not pay for the goods of which they take physical possession. Their goal is to collect products from the company and break bulk by storing them in a central location.

Distributors, Dealers, Stockists, and Agents

Some important characteristics of distributors include:

- They are required to invest in the product being bought from the company.
- They are on mark-up, margin and commission.
- They may or may not get credit from the company.
- Commission or margin is a percentage of the price at which they buy the product.
- Mark-up is the difference between the selling price of a good or service and cost. It is often expressed as a percentage over the cost.

Wholesalers

They normally operate out of the main markets. They usually deal with a large number of companies' products. They have their shops in busy trading areas. In some cases, wholesalers manage their margins on some products by selling empty cases. Their features are:

- They expand credit terms to their loyal customers.
- They can negotiate about 15 days' credit from distributors and special privileges on giving purchase requests.
- Their customers are other institutions, retailers and wholesalers.
- They are not on contract with any company.
- They choose and decide what products would be sold by them.

Retailers

They cater to the needs of hundreds of customers as they are the shopkeepers who set up shops in the marketplace. Retailer can command a lot of profitable terms from the distributors and companies when he is located in some part of the market that is very busy. Value added resellers purchase the incomplete kit or product and add value by selling to the customer depending on his specifications.

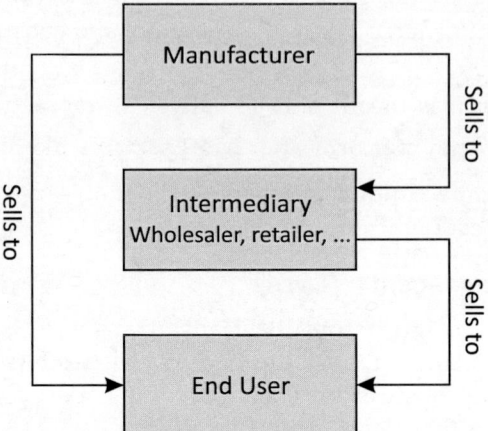

Figure 14.1 Retail Distribution Channel

Various Patterns of Distribution

After the selection of the most suitable channel of distribution, it is important to determine the intensity of desired distribution. There are three types of distribution intensity:

Selective

In this case only selected outlets are allowed to keep the company's products. The selection of outlets depends on the image that it wants to project regarding its exclusive products. For example, if someone is buying jewellery like Tanishq, it would be available in selective stores only. Selective distribution helps in keeping distribution costs lower and makes the product available in stores that matter most.

Intensive

This strategy makes sure that the product is available in as many stores as possible so that wherever the customer goes, he or she should be able to get the product as required.

This system is preferred by automobile manufacturers who require this intensity for their spare parts. In the FMCG sector also this system helps increase coverage and consequently sales. Three million outlets are available for the products of HLL and because of this, it is the best example of intensive distribution.

Exclusive

This is more selective than the selective distribution. The product may be stocked only by one outlet. In addition, the outlets set up by companies for their own products may also be counted, for example, Titan or Bata showrooms.

CASE STUDY

Electrical equipment is made by Genuine Motors which include generating sets, small transformers, pumps, motors etc. It has been doing business for the last 10 years and has established a brand name known for its quality. It has a factory located close to Chennai.

GM sells its products under the brand name Genuine in the Southern states of Andhra Pradesh, Kerala, Tamil Nadu and Karnataka. In Tamil Nadu and Karnataka, it has a dealer network and in the other 2 states wholesalers of electrical products help in selling. Andhra Pradesh and Kerala account for 60 percent of the business and other two states account for the remaining.

When GM first started in Andhra Pradesh and Kerala, it was difficult to find channel partners for the company. They recruited a set of 20 salespeople and started selling to business customers, wholesalers and retailers. The salespersons became experts in selling GM products which led to good output of the company.

When GM had to enter the markets of Tamil Nadu and Karnataka, they recruited about 4 salespersons for each of these states. They expected that the efforts would be made by wholesalers for distribution of goods to the rest of the market.

They had two kinds of channels in operation. Business was growing and current distribution had limited bandwidth and reach. Secondly, GM felt the need for a more robust distribution network in Tamil Nadu and Karnataka.

After 10 years of successfully running its business with the distribution effort focusing on salesmen, the company made the decision to use outside sources. They decided to recruit dealers in Andhra Pradesh and Kerala. There was low willingness among businessmen to become dealers. Thus, the offer of becoming a dealer was made to their salesman. They finally made two types of dealers: 1) businessmen who became dealers 2) salesmen who became dealers. The practice has been going on for 10 years with the same terms and conditions.

The experience of GM with both kinds of dealers has been different:

♦ Profitability was the main focus the businessmen dealers.

♦ Salesman turned dealers had good knowledge about products, competition, customers and markets which led to a know-it-all attitude.

♦ Any change in company policy was resisted by both the dealers.

GM wanted to build a strong distribution network in the states of Tamil Nadu and Karnataka. Instead of just relying on wholesalers for the 'reach', they relied on their distribution network. GM has the following options:

♦ Continue with wholesalers being serviced by company salesmen.

♦ Appoint dealers in all prominent and potential markets.

Questions

1. What are the pros and cons of continuing to work with wholesalers only?

2. If the decision is to appoint dealers, what should be the GM expectations from them?

SUMMARY

The management of all activities which facilitates movement and coordination of supply and demand in the creation of time and place utility in goodsis part of distribution management. Companies generally believe that distribution can best be performed by themselves and usually they undertake distribution related activities. There are various channels of distributions, each having its own unique characteristics. These include wholesalers, retailers, Carrying and Forwarding Agents, distributors, dealers, stockists, agents. After the selection of the most suitable channel of distribution, it is important to determine the intensity of desired distribution. They may be of three kinds: selective, intensive and exclusive. The goods may be distributed by different modes. There are several modes of transportation in the existing transport system. These include air, road, rail, and shipping.

KEY TERMS

Distribution management: Distribution management refers to the process of overseeing the movement of goods from supplier or manufacturer to point of sale.

Distribution channels: A distribution channel is a chain of businesses or intermediaries through which a good or service passes until it reaches the final buyer or the end consumer.

Wholesaler: A wholesaler is essentially a middleman between a manufacturer and a retail establishment.

Retailer: A retailer, or merchant, is an entity that sells goods such as clothing, groceries, or cars directly to consumers through various distribution channels with the goal of earning a profit.

EXERCISES

14.1 Define Distribution Management.

14.2 What are the various needs of distribution management?

14.3 Give an overview of various distribution channels.

14.4 Discuss the various patterns of distribution.

15

Designing Marketing Channels

INTRODUCTION

In order to deliver the expected customer service, an understanding of the types and functions of marketing channels must exist. Based on the structure of the channels required for meeting the needs of the customers, classification of the marketing channels is possible. It is also required to look at channel costs and how channel partners can sustain their business while delivering the expected levels of customer service.

MARKETING CHANNELS

The manufacturer is the originator of service and products. In the case of financial services, the product and service roles of the financial institutions are performed by making him appear to be a channel member. The end users also behave like channel members when they buy in large quantities instead of regular consumption.

CHANNEL LEVELS

The quantity of channel individuals chooses the degree of diverts in activity. A zero-channel means an immediate dispersion set-up where the item or administration is given to the end-client straight by the organisation.

A one-level channel comprises one go-between. For instance, an organisation might offer to the retailer who further offers to the clients.

The two-level channel would have two go-betweens. This is the most widely recognised for all FMCG organisations in India who have their own merchants who offer to retailers who administer the clients.

Option 1: Zero Levels (Direct distribution)

Option 2: One Level

Option 3: Two Level

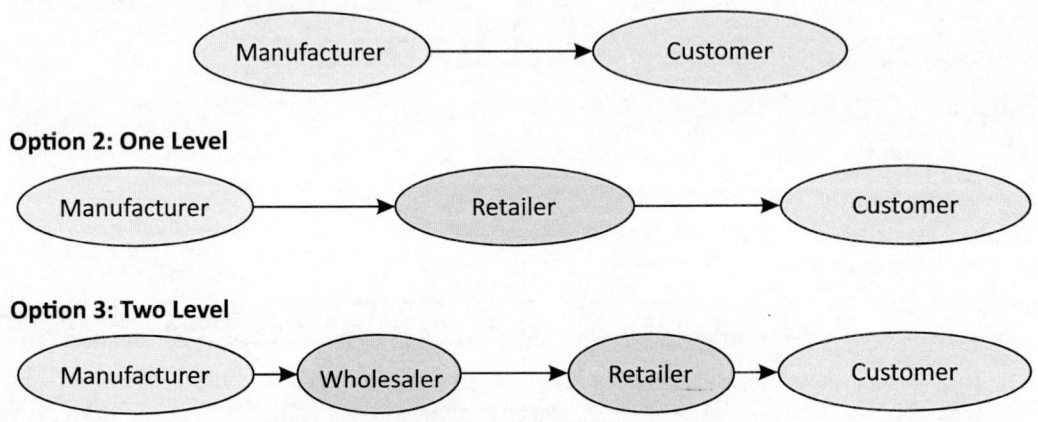

Figure 15.1 Levels of a Distribution Channel

CHANNEL FLOWS

Three kinds of flows are recognised which are as follows:

1. **Forward:** These are from the company to the customers, basically goods and services.
2. **Backward:** These are from customers to companies, mostly the value of goods and services bought by the customers.
3. **Both Ways Flow:** This is mainly information.

These three kinds of flows are broken down into following five flows:

♦ Promotion flow about consumer protection and the trade.
♦ Information flows about orders executed, orders placed and goods.
♦ Payment flow for goods.
♦ Title flow of goods.
♦ Physical flow of goods.

PROMINENT CHANNEL SYSTEMS

Vertical Marketing System

In this type of channel system each of the channel members act independently and try to run a business profitably. Vertical Marketing Systems are of three types:

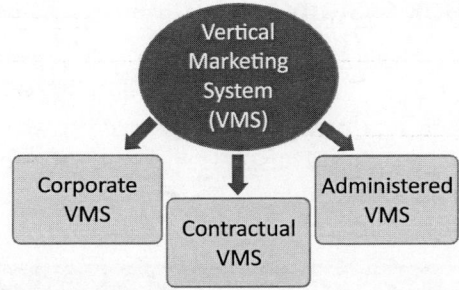

Figure 15.2 Vertical Marketing System

Corporate VMS

In this type of VMS, the successive stages of distribution and production are handled by a single entity. This provides a high degree of control to the company. Examples of companies that follow this system include: Bata, Bombay Dyeing, Titan, Raymond.

Administered VMS

The ownership of the distribution channel is not with a single entity but the single entity is of large influence. One usually large entity coordinates the distribution activities and gains market power by dominating the channel. Examples include Gillette, Coca-cola, Nestle.

Contractual VMS

A contractual VMS takes following forms:

♦ Wholesaler sponsored chains like Kemp toys.
♦ Retailer cooperatives where business entity is built to economies of scale.
♦ Manufacturer sponsored retail franchise.
♦ Manufacturer sponsored wholesaler franchise.

Horizontal Marketing System

This system operates between totally unrelated companies. But this kind of arrangement benefits both parties. They can exploit marketing opportunities better through this tie-up.

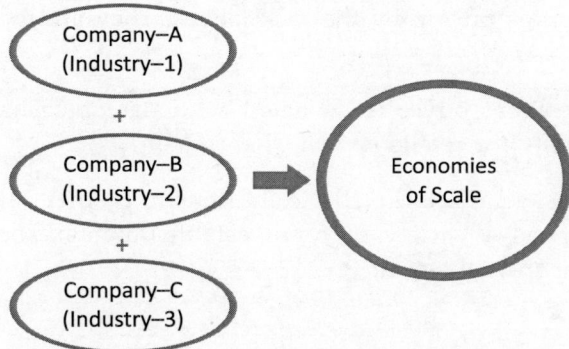

Figure 15.3 Horizontal Marketing System

Multi-channel Marketing Systems

This system is adopted by companies which use more than one marketing channel. The companies encourage their distributors to recruit new distributors for facilitating the sales of services and goods. It is a type of direct marketing where the sellers sell through referrals or word of mouth marketing. Thus, it is also known as network marketing, referral marketing or pyramid selling.

KINDS OF CHANNEL MEMBERS

The channels of distribution include buyer, producer and middlemen either retailer or wholesaler. The term middlemen refer to individuals and institutions who either negotiate or sell in the capacity of a broker or title of the goods. On the basis of taking title of goods these middlemen are divided into agent middlemen and merchant middlemen. Channel members are also classified into retailers and wholesalers. The various kind of middlemen are classified as below:

Agent: Title of goods is not taken by these middlemen known as agents. Active part is taken by them in rendering all services required through the marketing mechanism. Both seller and buyer are usually not represented by them in the same transaction. Examples include selling agent, manufacturer's agent and communication agent.

Broker: Brokers are the agents who represent either the seller or the buyer for the negotiation of sales and purchases as they do not have physical control directly of the goods they are dealing with. Usually, their powers are limited by the principal who decides terms of sales and prices.

Dealers: Firms that buy or sell goods on a wholesale or retail basis are known as dealers.

Distributors: This is a term synonymously used for wholesalers.

Rack Jobber: It includes a specialised line of merchandise as part of wholesaling business unit which markets to retail stores and provides special services such as stacking, maintenance and arrangement of products as display racks. Usually, the merchandise in the store of the retailers is put up by the rack jobber. They are the most common in the food business.

Resident Buyer: A resident buyer is an agent who has specialisation in buying on a commission or fee chiefly for retailers.

Retailers: Their business is to sell directly to the consumer; they may either be merchants or agents. A market has a variety of retail establishments. These are supermarkets, hypermarkets or departmental stores.

Figure 15.4   Retail

Wholesalers: They do not sell directly to ultimate consumers, rather it is a business unit which buys and resells merchandise to retailers or merchants or commercial, institutional or industrial buyers.

Figure 15.5   Wholesaler

Commission House: They are also known as commission merchants. They negotiate the sales of goods they handle and these agents usually exercise physical control over goods. As compared to brokers, the commission houses have broader power over the terms of sale, prices and methods. They usually remit the balance, collect producer's fee, extend necessary credit and arrange delivery.

Discount House: A discount house operates on a low scale and with minimum customer service. It can be called a retailing business unit that features durable consumer units that compete on the basis of price appeal.

Branch House: It is detached from the head office and the manufacturer usually maintains this establishment. It is used for the purchase of servicing, delivering, selling and stocking the product. A branch house is the same as a branch office.

Facilitating Agencies: These agencies assist or perform in assisting the performance of marketing functions. Common types include advertising agencies, insurance companies, commodity exchanges, warehouses, railways and banks.

Consumer Cooperative: A retail business operated and owned by ultimate consumers for distributing and purchasing services and goods primarily to the members are sometimes referred as purchase cooperatives.

Industrial Store: Company stores are operated and owned by companies to sell to governmental establishments or own employees.

Figure 15.6 Industrial Store

NEED FOR SELECTING CHANNEL MEMBERS

Among the most crucial decisions that a company has to take are the decisions relating to marketing channels. Sometimes companies do not have sufficient information regarding the number of channel members, locations and types. Due to this lack of information companies tend to make wrong decisions related to development of channels. The pricing of companies depends on whether they use selective or extensive distribution. The need for decisions related to channels is felt more in the case when:

(a) A new product or line of product is introduced by a company

(b) An existing product is aimed at a new target market.

(c) There is a huge change in the environment.

Besides the above-mentioned factors, the understanding of when, how, where and what consumers buy in a market selected by manufacturer is also helpful in designing market channels. Thus, consideration should be given to aggregate demand of each product as well as service output by the average consumer.

FACTORS CONSIDERED IN SELECTING CHANNELS

Usually, after considering the effectiveness and efficiency of the distribution channel, the manufacturer selects the channels that are cost effective. There are various factors that need to be considered before selecting the channel which are as follows:

Nature of Market

The requirement of what the consumer wants and how much is wanted helps in the selection of channels. It is also required that the manufacturer himself determines what he wants. It is required to assess competition, scope of distribution, seasonality of sales, repeat sales, concentration of purchases, size of average sale and paying habits of consumers.

Nature of Products

Perishability: Due to the dangers associated with repeated handling and delays there is a requirement of direct marketing for perishable products.

Size: Short channels are required in case of products that are bulky so that number and distance of handling from producer to consumer can be reduced.

Style: It is preferred by manufacturers to sell directly to retailers when there are fast changes in style of goods.

Unit Value: High unit value products are usually sold through the company's own sales forces rather than middlemen.

Newness: New channels are preferred in case of new products after introduction.

Consumer's Buying Habits

Size of Average Sale: The channels should be elaborate when the quantity sold is small.

Seasonal Character: The distribution of seasonal goods must be done on a continuous basis even though they will have only seasonal marketing.

Concentration of Customers: Direct selling would be beneficial when the localised and concentrated market exists.

Competition: Careful consideration and thorough analysis of this factor is required. Most of the competitors prefer similar types of channels. This is done for two reasons, firstly, channels would be familiar and it would be easy to reach customers. Secondly, using totally different channels would increase the cost of distribution and may even impact sales.

Financial Consideration: This is mainly done to come over any of the difficulties that may arise temporary and seasonal goods.

Cost of Channel: The higher cost of channels would ultimately be reflected in the cost of the product. Distribution arranged through middlemen is generally economical whereas direct marketing is costly.

DISTRIBUTION POLICIES AND STRATEGIES

Economy and effectiveness in serving the customer should be the ultimate aim of a policy. The major four decisions that ought to be made in this context are:

- ♦ **Channel Length:** This includes decisions related to choose a retailer, middlemen, wholesaler or some other combination.
- ♦ **Channel Number:** This involves the choice of different marketing channels that can be employed.
- ♦ **Channel Member Type:** The kinds of retailers, middlemen and wholesalers that should be brought in.
- ♦ **Channel Width:** At each level of the channel, how many individual firms and outlets that can be employed. The width of the channel is chosen from among the following three alternatives:
  - (i) Intensive distribution
  - (ii) Selective distribution
  - (iii) Exclusive distribution

SHOULD MIDDLEMEN BE ELIMINATED

Certain philosophers have advocated the existence/elimination of middlemen through following arguments:

1. The chain of distribution is unnecessarily lengthened by the addition of middlemen. They add to the cost of marketing by increasing the number of intermediaries between consumers and manufacturers. This results in an increase of the final price paid by the customers. The profit of middlemen comes from the margin of profit added by them to the price of the product.

2. The risks associated with production are not borne by the middlemen. The industrial risks arise out of fluctuations like recession and depression, shortage of raw materials, power failures or strikes. The intermediaries are not affected by these risks in any way.

3. The work of most middlemen is mainly of transfer agents. Any significant marketing function is not performed by the middlemen through whose hands most of the goods are passed on. Such middlemen hinder the good flow from producers to the consumers. The goods would reach the consumers at less cost and more quickly if the unnecessary intermediaries are removed.

4. Middlemen usually have a tendency to exploit situations for their own profits rather than taking any risks upon themselves as has been seen in general practice. Retailers and wholesalers allegedly create artificial scarcity and try to earn profits at the cost of customers and society in general.

5. Middlemen stock the goods of different manufacturers. They have a tendency to promote the goods of those producers who make better offers to them in terms and conditions of agreement.

6. Since, with the advancement in communication and transportation systems, the modes of transport have become regular and fast that there is no problem in sending the goods to any corner of the country without delay. This has only been possible due to extensive and rapid development of communication and transport systems.

SPECIAL DISTRIBUTION METHODS

Consignment Selling: The practice of placing goods in the hands of middlemen is part of consignment selling. Usually, the retailers and wholesalers retain the position of agents as the title and the control remain with the seller. The retailers and wholesalers only get a commission on the sales effected through them. Even when the distribution is in the hands of others, the manufacturer who owns the goods specifies the price of the product, time and manner of sale. This shows that the control is retained by the manufacturer over his merchandise. However, nowadays this kind of distribution is not found.

Franchise Selling: This method is not a widely used method of distribution as is typically American in origin. In this method the required machinery for selling is provided by the manufacturer who arranges the distribution through some individual outlets. This method is beneficial when the manufacturer lacks the knowledge of marketing and capital for the products.

Symbiotic Marketing: This method is new in comparison to others. Under this method, in order to exploit new opportunities, two or more companies develop a joint marketing strategy. For instance, a product may have been developed by a company and it may still lack the channel of distribution for reaching the target market. They do symbiotic marketing by joining hands. The symbiotic marketing may be the result of lack of marketing knowledge, lack of capital or changing patterns of distribution.

CASE STUDY

IWalk 2.0—Medical/AT Device Distribution Network with Intense Clinician Training Support from the Manufacturer

Hands Free crutch is a modified crutch for people with lower leg non-weight-bearing injuries. It supports the injured leg from the knee down with the person's weight resting on the knee of their bent, injured leg. It enables a person to walk much like a peg legged pirate did in olden times.

Individuals with lower leg non-weight-bearing wounds who wish to stay walking have long utilised standard braces. The utilisation of standard braces is predicated on one's capacity to utilize their arms and hands to help their weight as they explore around in their environmental elements. The utilisation of standard braces doesn't permit the free utilisation of your hands and arms for different exercises. It was noticed that there was a requirement for a gadget that permitted one to stay mobile regardless of the free utilisation of their arms and hands.

The iWalk 2.0 was created as such a gadget and is a hands-free support substitute (iWalk-Free, n.d.). It is a first of its kind versatility gadget that liberates an individual from the limits of ordinary bolsters. Instead of promoting this new gadget straightforwardly to the buyer, the organisation chose to market the gadget straightforwardly to clinicians who might normally be fitting the objective populace with standard props.

Normal misinterpretations from simply taking a gander at the iWalk 2.0 territory from that it is unsound and you might be harmed utilizing it, to that it will be challenging to learn and utilise. So how could this be tended to for both the clinician and the shopper? In the first place, the organisation gave an exceptionally useful site to act as a source of perspective for the clinicians and customers. Then, the organisation actually shows every retailer the gadget, how to sell it, and how to fit it. The organisation gives an online class and ensures clinicians (vendors) to become iWalk fitters. The item ordinarily outflanks purchaser assumptions, so the vendor must be furnished with the information to incapacitate customer confusions.

The iWalk 2.0 dispersion channel is that of being sold by the producer straightforwardly to prepared vendors who thus sell the buyer on the item. There is no advancement methodology other than going into new clinical gadget rivalries at different career expos all through the country and winning them. The iWalk 2.0 has additionally profited from exposure on its utilisation by high profile figures, for example, Harrison Ford. Mr. Ford utilizes the iWalk 2.0 because of a physical issue he caused during shooting of the new Star Wars film.

Question

1. What is the best way of informing your target market of your product's existence?

SUMMARY

The manufacturer is the originator of service and products. In the case of financial services, the product and service roles of the financial institutions are performed by making him appear to be a channel member. There are prominently three kinds of channel systems: vertical marketing system, horizontal marketing system and multi-channel marketing system. The channels of distribution include buyer, producer and middlemen either retailer or wholesaler. Among the most crucial decisions that a company has to take are the decisions relating to marketing channels. Sometimes companies do not have sufficient information regarding the number of channel members, locations and types. Usually, after considering the effectiveness and efficiency of the distribution channel, the manufacturer selects the channels that is cost effective. Economy and effectiveness in serving the customer should be the ultimate aim of a policy.

KEY TERMS

Consignment selling: The practice of placing goods in the hands of middlemen is part of consignment selling.

Franchise selling: This method is not a widely used method of distribution as is typically American in origin.

Horizontal marketing system: It is a form of distribution channel wherein two or more companies at the same level unrelated to each other come together to gain the economies of scale.

Multi-channel marketing system: It is the marketing strategy wherein the direct sales companies encourage its existing distributors to recruit new distributors to facilitate the sale of goods and services.

Symbiotic marketing: This method is new in comparison to others. Under this method, in order to exploit new opportunities, two or more companies develop a joint marketing strategy.

Vertical marketing system: It comprises the main distribution channel partners—the producer, the wholesaler and the retailer who work together as a unified group to serve the customer needs.

EXERCISES

15.1 What are the different channel levels and channel flows?

15.2 Describe the three prominent channel systems.

15.3 What are the different methods of direct marketing and when should they be used?

15.4 What is the role of a wholesaler? How does he help in promoting sales?

15.5 What are the criteria for selecting the dealer and the intermediaries?

15.6 Explain why middlemen should be eliminated.

16

Channel Institutions
Retailing

INTRODUCTION

Retailing refers to "all activities involved in selling or renting consumer products and services directly to ultimate consumers for their personal or household use". In addition to selling, activities such as maintaining inventory, data processing, advertising and buying are included in retailing.

> "Retailing includes all the activities involved in selling goods or services directly to final consumers for their personal, non-business use". A retail organisation is "any organisation that is involved in this type of selling irrespective of how and where goods and services are being sold". A retailer is "the person or an organisation who is involved in these type of activities".
>
> —Philip Kotler

Sale of consumer products or industrial products is not included in retailing. Further, all firms engaged in retailing cannot be called retailers. It can be said that a retailer "is the person or a firm that derives more than half of its sales revenue from sales made directly to ultimate consumers".

Some common definitions of retailing are as follows:

Retailing includes all activities directly related to sale of goods or services to the ultimate consumer for personal and non-business use.

—Stanton

Retailing is selling final consumer products to households.

—McCarthy

Retailing consists of activities involved in selling directly to the ultimate consumer.

—Cundiff and Still

The primary strategies for retailers revolve around four operational elements:

♦ First is concerning inventory and margin turnover rates. High emphasis is placed on minimum service operation, high turnover and low margin.

♦ The second element concerns assortments and variety whereby retailing institutions evolve and design product mix strategies to suit the changing patterns of shopping.

♦ The third element focuses on convenience and location. Although the emphasis is on convenience, the trade-off between spatial convenience for lines of trade and one-stop shopping convenience is difficult.

♦ The fourth element is customer service. Large retailers have divided their market into segments with low, moderate and high service requirements.

FUNCTIONS OF RETAILING

1. **Physical Possession Flow:**
   ♦ Passing the delivery goods to customers for a price.
   ♦ Maintaining desired assortments in both required quantity and variety for supplying to customers.
   ♦ Maintaining storage facilities.
   ♦ Taking possession of goods from wholesalers.

2. **Title:** Passing the title of goods to customers after taking it from manufacturers or wholesalers.

3. **Promotion:** Participating in the manufacturer's promotion programme by acting as final dispensers of sales promotion schemes and organising point of purchase and store display.

4. **Negotiation:** Negotiating with manufacturers and wholesalers over quantity, quality and price as well as terms of sale. This also includes negotiating terms of sale and price with customers.

5. **Finance:** Retailers sometimes agree to sell on credit to finance ultimate consumers. In small villages and towns retailers play a powerful role by acting as creditor for day to day and monthly purchases.

6. **Risk Bearing:** Ownership is accompanied by risks. All the risk inherent in ownership of goods is assumed by retailers. As in the case of wholesalers, risk

may be offset by manufacturers or wholesalers' willingness to accept returned stocks.

7. **Order Flow:** In anticipation of the needs of customers, retailers direct the backward flow of orders to the manufacturer through the wholesaler.

8. **Payment Flow:** Accepting payments from customers in consideration for the transfer of ownership retailers pass on the payment backward in the channel.

9. **Information Flow:** In the two-way flow, retailers form a vital link. They disseminate promotional and product information to the customers and on the other hand they share problems, complaints, satisfaction and dissatisfaction of customers to manufacturers.

IMPORTANCE OF RETAILING

When producers sell directly to their final buyers in an organisation marketing then they get linked to their final buyer in marketing channels. In consumer product marketing such types of direct channels are not commonly available. Most of the purchases are made by the consumers at the retail stores which work independently of the producer. Thus, the final stage for consumer products in a marketing channel is retailing. They provide the most important link between the ultimate consumers and the producers. The simple selling and buying does not encompass the entire retailing. Since economic utility is created by it, therefore, it is important for consumers. On the other hand, as it forms the most important connection between the end-users and the manufacturers, it is important to them.

CLASSIFICATION OF RETAILERS

1. **On the basis of their conventional understanding of the retail practices in the Indian context**

   ♦ *Limited line retailers:* specialize in line of products that are related.

   ♦ *General stores:* anything which can be sold in reasonable volume is carried in such stores.

   ♦ *Conventional stores:* such stores work on price competition avoidance.

2. **On the basis of expanded service and assortment**

   ♦ *Department store:* combining speciality shops and limited line retailers.

   ♦ *Speciality shops:* special types of products are sold there like sporting goods.

3. **On the basis of mass merchandising retailers**

   ♦ *Hypermarkets:* all goods and services that are purchased routinely and very large in size that try to carry items other than drugs and food.

   ♦ *Mass merchandisers:* stores that focus on high turnover and low margins with many departments having self-service stores.

   ♦ *Discount houses:* at substantial price cuts a wide assortment is offered.

Figure 16.1 Hypermarket

♦ *Catalogue showroom retailers:* display showroom with back-up inventories and sell several lines out of a catalogue.

♦ *Supermarkets:* large stores specializing in self-service and wide assortment including grocery.

Figure 16.2 Supermarket

4. **Based on added convenience**
   ♦ Telephone and direct mail retailing.
   ♦ Selling directly at the consumer's home through door-to-door.
   ♦ *Automatic vending:* delivering and selling products through machines.
   ♦ *Convenience stores:* limited line food stores offering convenience and not assortment.

Evolution of Retailing

The history of retailing can be said to be very old. It started from small one-man owned stores to the discount and department stores found in a modern world. In urban areas such department and discount stores have come up in abundance but in rural areas, general stores still exist. Therefore, several theories have been proposed to explain the continuous evolution of retailing. These are as follows:

The Wheel of Retailing

In 1958, Malcolm P McNair, a Professor from Harvard explained the retailing evolution. It came to be known as the wheel of retailing. This theory includes the cyclical patterns of vulnerability, trading up and innovation. As per this theory, any retailer enters the market with a limited product line, low margins and low prices. As the innovator is able to attract customers from established retailers, he rises to copy the innovators. This forces the previous retailers to trade up by adding more services, opening fancier stores and expanding product lines. The original innovator may be challenged when lower profit is initially accepted by new entrants.

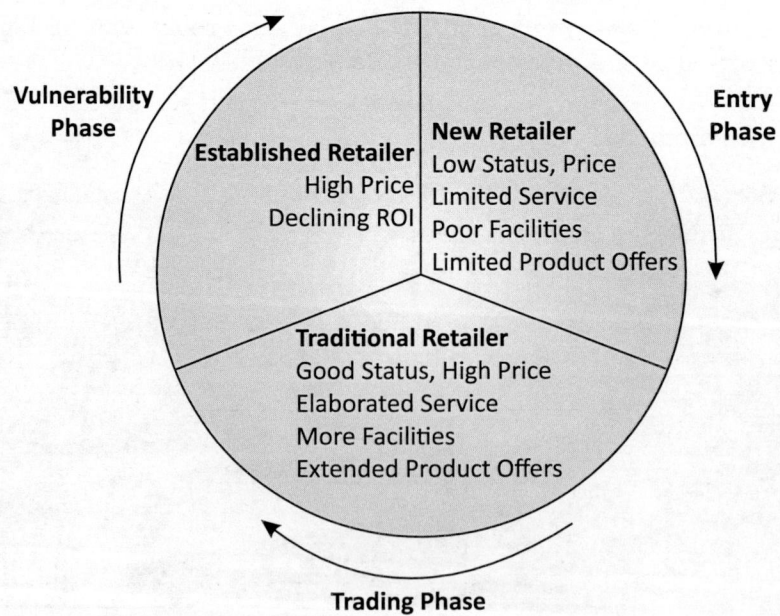

Figure 16.3 Wheel of Retailing

The Dialectic Process

To explain the changes that occur in retailing, another theory has been proposed that is known as the dialectic process. As per this theory, when a new competitor in order to gain competitive advantage uses an innovation then the established retailer will use a strategy that brings it closer to the innovation. Some of the innovator's appeal is negated by the established retailer by making the innovation as his own. Generally, by modifying original retail concepts, adding or upgrading product lines, competitive advantage can be gained.

The Retail Life Cycle

Retail life cycle is the third theory in the evolution of retailing. This theory states that retailers undergo four different stages: introduction, growth, maturity and decline. The first stage of introduction starts when a retailer establishes his store. In the growth stage, the retailer adds new product lines and competitive advantage. The third stage of maturity comes when sales reach a plateau and growth slows. The retailer cuts prices and fights for market share during this stage. In present times the retailer moves from introduction to maturity stage at a very fast pace.

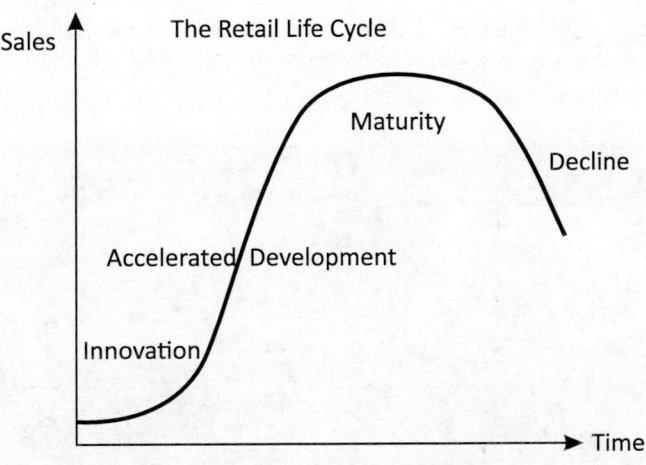

Figure 16.4   Retail Life Cycle

Types of Utility in Retailing

There are mainly four types of utility which are discussed in the following paragraphs:

Form Utility

This type of utility includes the service or design of the product. The form utility will be higher when a commodity is produced based on the requirements and desires of the customers. In simple words, by translating customer's requirements into needed goods and services, form utility can be achieved. In order to do this, observing customers in the target areas is the best technique which makes it happen easily.

For example, when a motorcycle company named Elite Bikes is considered. It can sell the parts separately but instead it assembles and presents the whole vehicle. This is done to increase the form utility and it adds value derived by consumers.

Place Utility

Place utility can be acquired by providing easy access to services and goods. Consumers get attracted to a product that can be purchased without much hassle. Generally, the distribution medium helps in deciding the place utility of a product. It is also influenced by a product's availability in the digital market.

In the earlier example, if Elite Bikes is only sold in India, then it would not seem an attractive option to people in Singapore. However, if the bikes are sold globally then it would be a lucrative choice.

Time Utility

When a product is made available as soon as the need arises then the time utility exists. There should be fast availability of a product. When a product or service is scarce then time utility is high. Because of the various processes involved in supply chain management like delivery, storage and logistics; it has a substantial impact on time utility.

For example, car rental services like Ola and Uber can increase time utility by providing services based on the urgency of customers.

Figure 16.5   Time Utility Provided by Taxi Services

Possession Utility

The gain and satisfaction received from having and using a particular good or service. Enhanced possession utility is held by useful products. Renting contracts and credit cards are the acquisition processes through which it is done. A utility is perceived highly when it is acquired easily.

For example, when repair services cannot be availed by someone who is experiencing a problem in his Air Conditioner. Possession utility is increased in case when AC is fixed within agreeable time by the AC company.

RETAILING SCENARIO IN INDIA

It is estimated that there are over 12 million retail outlets in India of different varieties and sizes. This works out to over 10 outlets per 1000 population. The unorganised sector, which has many independent, small stores contributing to about 96 per cent of the retailing business. The average per capita space for retail in India is 2 square feet compared to 15 square feet in the US. This is in line with the population of India itself which is dispersed. Moreover, nearly three-fourth of the population is rural in hundreds of small villages that cannot support bigger retail formats.

Some features of retail industry in India are as follows:

- Total domestic retail market is estimated at ₹9300 billion and growing at 3 to 4% per annum.
- An estimated 32.9 lakh retailers having around 60 lakh sales persons exist in India.
- Out of these, nearly 21 lakhs are involved in selling non-durable goods.
- Majority of the retailers belong to cities and only one-third exist in villages.
- In India, an estimated six retailers exist per one thousand population whereas in the USA seven retailers for every 1000 persons.

Rural India

Some features of rural markets include:

- Rural markets generally stock regional and local brands with longer credit periods and higher margins
- An estimated 50 per cent of rural population prefers buying from weekly haats or shanties
- Poor reach of media and communication, poor visibility and product display, poor storage system, low density of shops per village,
- Dispersed trade and population, poor road connectivity and large number of small markets.

ONLINE RETAILING OR E-TAILING

As the name suggests, electronic retailing is shopping on the Internet without the consumer having to visit a physical store. It has the following advantages:

- A favourable image is created for the company.
- Promotion of new products or services and use of demonstrations to highlight features.

♦ Provides details of loyalty programmes, answer to queries, price comparisons, choices available and product information.

♦ Reaches consumers anywhere in the world.

CASE STUDY

Indian Retailing: India is an underexplored retail market, where over 90% of the business is under unorganised retailers. However, with the arising retail market, the potential is enormous. The informed, hopeful working-class Indian buyers, with inclinations vigorously shifted towards spending than saving, are a promising option for the greater part of the retailers. This makes India appealing to both the Indian corporate houses and the unfamiliar players.

Walmart-Bharti Retail Alliance: The Best Strategy? India's true capacity and positive socioeconomics had become popular in the past and retailers all over the planet need to get into the market. However, the retailing industry in India is exceptionally secured and is majorly dominated by advantageous neighbourhood kirana stores. The unfamiliar retailers have found an open door since the public authority has chosen to open up for FDI. From the time 100 per cent FDI was permitted in real money and convey discount, unfamiliar firms have chosen to enter India. Discount turns into a decent choice for the huge retailers who intend to enter India.

Three alternatives were suggested for the joint venture as follows:

Alternative 1: Through changing the strategic orientation, Walmart planned to open hundreds of stores but later dropped the idea. Walmart opened just five stores when it planned to open 22 stores. Since Walmart struggled to gain market share, the expansion plan needed to be reconsidered.

Alternative 2: Improve corporate image through corporate social responsibility. Walmart was blamed for creating unemployment by removing local businesses. Walmart planned to remove this stereotype by launching a local campaign to fulfil social responsibility in agriculture and education. Therefore, it would require both parties to spend an extra amount on the campaigns.

Alternative 3: Doing separate business would be another alternative. Bharti enterprise struggled in its business as it was under a heavy debt. Bharti retail's liquidity would affect the ability of the joint venture to pay for its financial obligations.

Questions

1. Which is the best strategy for FDI in retailing?
2. Which alternative should the companies choose?

SUMMARY

Retailing includes all activities involved in selling or renting consumer products and services directly to ultimate consumers for their personal or household use. Sale of consumer products or industrial products is not included in retailing. Further, all firms engaged in retailing cannot be called retailers. It can be said that a retailer is the person or a firm that derives more than half of its sales revenue from sales made directly to ultimate consumers. Retailers are classified into different categories based on service, assortment, mass merchandising, retail practices and convenience.

KEY TERMS

Discount stores: A discount store or discounter offers a retail format in which products are sold at prices that are in principle lower than an actual or supposed "full retail price".

e-tailing: It is the selling of retail goods on the Internet.

Hypermarkets: A hypermarket is a retail store that combines a department store and a grocery supermarket.

Supermarkets: A supermarket is a self-service shop offering a wide variety of food, beverages and household products, organised into sections.

Retailing: Retailing includes all the activities involved in selling goods or services directly to final consumers for their personal, non-business use.

EXERCISES

16.1 How does retailing help in the function of selling?

16.2 How is a retailer different from a wholesaler?

16.3 What are the implications of retailer power for channel management in case of the following products:
   (i) Unbranded electrical appliances,
   (ii) A locally made detergent powder.

16.4 What are the various types of utility in retailing?

16.5 Discuss online retailing in detail.

17

Channel Institutions
Wholesaling

INTRODUCTION

The requirement of wholesalers rose because reaching a large number of customers requires a large number of retailers. Therefore, reaching so many retailers is not possible for the company alone because they require channel intermediary in the form of a wholesaler. There are two types of wholesalers which include distributors or dealers and freelance wholesalers.

IMPORTANT DEFINITIONS OF WHOLESALING

Wholesaling includes "all the activities in selling goods or services to those who buy for resale or business use.
—Philip Kotler

Wholesalers buy and resale merchandise to retailers and other merchants and to industrial, institutional and commercial users, but do not sell in significant amounts to ultimate consumers.   —Cundiff and Still

A person or firms that buy merchandise and resell it either to retailers for subsequent resale to the consumer or to business firms for industrial and business use is called a wholesaler.   —Mason and Ratch

Wholesalers are defined as "people who sell to retailers or other merchants and industrial, institutional and commercial users but they do not sell in significant amounts to ultimate consumers."
—American Marketing Association

WHOLESALER VS. RETAILER

Basis for Comparison	Wholesale	Retail
Meaning	Wholesale is a business in which goods are sold in large quantities to the retailers, industries and other businesses.	When the goods are sold to the final consumer in small lots, then this type of business is termed as retail.
Creates link between	Manufacturer and Retailer	Wholesaler and Customer
Price	Lower	Comparatively higher
Competition	Less	Very high
Volume of transaction	Large	Small
Capital Requirement	Huge	Little
Deals in	Limited products	Different products
Area of operation	Extended to various cities	Limited to a specific area
Art of selling	Not Required	Required
Need for advertisement	No	Yes

Source: Surbhi, 2018 (https://keydifferences.com/difference-between-wholesale-and-retail.html)

FUNCTIONS OF WHOLESALERS

There are two main functions of wholesalers based on the following types:

Merchant wholesalers: These merchants buy goods in bulk and resell them to consumers for a profit, firstly, reselling the goods again to someone else and secondly, consuming the goods in the course of operation of a profit-making enterprise. The profit made on the sale of a good is the compensation for a merchant wholesaler.

Service wholesaler: These are traditional wholesalers by whom most of the marketing functions are performed which are generally associated with wholesaling. They participate in all or most of marketing flows and are especially useful for broad retail lines like drugs and groceries.

They perform following functions:

♦ **Physical Possession Flow**

  (i) Delivering goods to customer.

(ii) Maintaining stocks of goods in both quantity and variety for supplying to customers on regular basis.

(iii) Maintaining storage facilities.

(iv) Taking possession of goods.

♦ **Ownership Flow:** Taking legal ownership from the supplier and passing it on to customers when sale is made.

♦ **Promotion:** Participating in manufacturer's advertising allowances, printing catalogues for trade and advertising to trade and maintaining sales force.

♦ **Negotiation:** Making contact and negotiating over terms of sale, quantity, quality and prices with both customers and suppliers.

♦ **Risk Taking:** Assuming risks of failure after taking ownership and of changes in price of the goods. Risk assumption may be offset by manufacturers willingness to accept guarantee prices or returns.

♦ **Ordering:** Flow of ordering moves from retailer to manufacturer. In real life, they anticipate the needs of retailers and order from manufacturers in advance of actual sales to retailers.

♦ **Payment:** Accepting payment for goods from customers, paying supplier before collecting from the customer and passing payment minus expenses and profit to the supplier.

SELECTING OF WHOLESALERS

The criteria involve the following steps:

♦ Identification of two or three prospects for each appointment based on requirements of the company.

♦ Checking the background of each candidate that is shortlisted.

♦ Finding out the interest levels by meeting the prospects and explaining the requirements to them.

♦ One or two final candidates have to be shortlisted after getting all the information.

♦ Final selection is made on quantitative and qualitative factors. The qualitative factors could be keeping the image of the company, willingness to abide by rules, willingness to spend time in the market, confidence in himself and company products.

The candidate with the highest score gets selected. The entire process of selection must be without bias.

Based on his performance evaluation a wholesaler is selected. The following questions need to be analysed before selecting wholesalers:

♦ How can business users be served by wholesalers?

♦ How can retailers be served by wholesalers?

♦ How can suppliers be served by wholesalers?

Key Tasks of Wholesalers

In order to discharge their responsibilities, the wholesalers execute the following key tasks:

- ◆ **Aggregation of Goods:** The wholesaler is generally very clear at the start of this task regarding the requirements of his set of customers. He is aware of the quantity and quality of the goods needed by his customers. Hence, wholesalers can place orders to their suppliers who can be other wholesalers or producers.

- ◆ **Warehousing of Goods:** Protection of goods is the responsibility of the wholesaler after he has bought them from a distributor. For the quantities the wholesaler buys, he has to make sure that he has safe and adequate storage space. The warehouse may be rented or his own. The goods may even be insured depending on the value of the goods. The distributor must provide good storage facilities when the goods that need to be stored in temperature-controlled conditions.

- ◆ **Booking of Orders:** For selling the goods already bought, the wholesaler has to book orders regularly from his customers.

- ◆ **Transporting of Goods:** Goods are rarely delivered by freelance wholesalers at the doorstep of their customers. Usually, they reach the shop for placing orders and collection of goods.

- ◆ **Financing of Business:** For buying the goods that a wholesaler wants to sell, finance has to be provided. Credit facility is rarely extended by companies to distributors or wholesalers.

- ◆ **Bearing of Risks:** For the stocks that the wholesaler is trying to sell, he has already paid in advance. While in possession of the stocks, the wholesaler is responsible for any losses.

- ◆ **Packing and Grading:** The wholesaler sells to his customers in small sizes by breaking the bulk. Some re-packing may have to be done for this.

- ◆ **Providing Marketing Information:** He is a two-way communicator of information that is valuable. He informs various types of goods available, promotions in force and competition to his retail customers.

CLASSIFICATION OF WHOLESALERS

There are basically three types of wholesale institutions:

Merchant Wholesalers

Ownership of goods that they deal with is taken by merchant wholesalers. Merchant wholesalers are independently owned separate from retailers on one hand and suppliers on the other hand. The most distinguishable feature of the merchant wholesalers is that they take ownership of goods and the risks associated with them. Generally, merchant wholesalers are of two types:

1. Full function
2. Limited function

Full Function: These wholesalers are known as jobbers or distributors also. The functions normally associated with wholesaling like marketing functions are performed by these wholesalers. A broad variety of goods are carried by them.

Limited Function: Some of the functions typically associated with wholesaling are performed by these wholesalers. The most common type of limited function wholesalers are:

- *Cash and Carry Wholesalers:* No delivery on credit is offered by these wholesalers to their small business customers. Neither do they provide any managerial assistance to their customers.

- *Drop Shippers:* The possession of goods handled by them is not taken by such wholesalers. Drop shippers generally market commodities like natural resources, for example, coal and commodities like grains.

- *Truck Wholesalers:* As their inventories are carried on their trucks so limited functions are performed by these wholesalers. A high degree of locational convenience is provided by these wholesalers to their customers.

- *Mail Order Wholesalers:* Similar to mail order retailers, these wholesalers also perform their functions.

- *Producer's Cooperatives:* Producer cooperatives are owned by people who produce similar types of goods or services.

- *Rack Jobbers:* A rack jobber is a company or trader that has an agreement with a retailer to display and sell products in a store.

Agent Wholesalers

Agent wholesalers do not take ownership unlike merchant wholesalers. They market the products that they take possession of from producers. They are involved in the selling and buying of services and goods. They also participate in the ordering, promotion and collection of market information. Among various such agents are auction companies, selling agents, commission merchants, brokers and manufacturer's agents. Agent wholesalers play a major role in both international and domestic trade.

Manufacturer's Agents

These are independent firms used in place of the manufacturer's own sales force and which handle non-competing lines of a variety of manufacturers. New companies use manufacturer's agents when they have neither the resources nor the expertise for developing their own sales force. When firms wish to sub-contract their distribution strategies and wish to only concentrate upon manufacturing then they rely on manufacturer's agents.

STRATEGIC MANAGEMENT OF WHOLESALERS

The following major factors are important for the success of a wholesaler's firm:

New Technology: Relations with both suppliers and customers are strengthened with automation and mechanisation. In today's scenario, new technology has greater significance in wholesaling business.

Proprietary Brands: For maintaining and gaining a sustained competitive advantage, wholesalers develop strong proprietary brands.

Niche Marketing: Niche marketing strategies are followed by several retailers who specialize in unique or limited product categories.

Profitability: There are two factors on which the profitability of wholesalers is based:

1. Achieving high rates of assets turnover.
2. Managing net profit margins

Effectiveness: The wholesaler's effectiveness depends on

1. Changes in the target market are met by adjustment of product and service mix
2. Satisfying needs through product and service mix
3. Identification of target market needs

WHOLESALING IN INDIA

The wholesaler is the most likely middleman who is targeted by customers and companies alike. A freelance wholesaler does not have friends in the companies whereas in case of its own distributors the roles are clearly defined. As 75% of the Indian population lives in rural areas, the freelance wholesalers will exist for a long period of time.

The freelance wholesalers have various number of factors in their favour for continuing operations:

♦ Visiting wholesale mandis is the only option for retailers to purchase pulses, cereals and food grains and in the process, a lot of goods are sold by the wholesalers.

♦ Wholesalers extend credit to their customers which companies are never able to match.

♦ There is no organised distribution network in the case of vegetables, fruits and grains.

♦ To get big sales volumes even big companies need wholesalers.

♦ Hundreds of companies depend entirely on wholesalers and cannot afford their own distribution networks.

♦ There are coverage limitations for companies which are made up by wholesalers.

Rural Markets

The market within 20–25 km of radius of the distributor is expected to be developed by him. Initially these markets may not be able to be on beat plan but as soon as salespeople are able to work the markets and business stabilises, he would look for better territory coverage within the allotted time. The company salespeople initiate the visits to these markets. Care must be taken that markets already on the beat plan of an adjacent distributor must not be targeted.

CASE STUDY

A national wholesale distributor supply was attempting to deal with its complicated inventory network and keep up with elevated degrees of client support. With a total of 20 decentralised destinations spread across five states, conveying conveyance needs between sales staff, proficient drivers was made difficulty.

Intensifying the issues, Department of Transportation indulgence affected the wholesaler's capacity to meet its clients' conveyance needs and increased risk. The merchant went to Logistics to help smooth out and work on its conveyances to stockrooms, houses, places of work, lofts, and organisations. The organisation has permitted the merchant to further develop customer assistance, decrease the size of its in-house armada and tap into committed limit. Using ability likewise empowered the wholesaler to focus on its main business as opposed to transportation concerns.

The merchant's parent organisation involves transportation-as-a-cost-of-deals as a measurement to look at specialty units, so it is basic to oversee costs. ClearChain innovation permits clients to unify their information, seeing and understanding their complete transportation spend. The innovation has likewise enhanced the organisation and smooth out conveyances, driving in general expense reserve funds.

In addition, the merchant saw added esteem with proficient, proficient drivers who showed up on time at its clients' locales. As a component of its correspondence, colleagues from Logistics and the merchant meet routinely to examine measurements, information examination, needs, and plans. The expanded perceivability empowers information driven navigation, and ordinary gatherings give the two players clear bearings for what's in store.

Question
1. How can transportation costs be managed for technology driven wholesalers?

SUMMARY

Wholesalers buy and resale merchandise to retailers and other merchants and to industrial, institutional and commercial users, but do not sell in significant amount to ultimate consumer. There are two main functions of wholesalers based on their types—merchant wholesalers and service wholesalers. Based on his performance evaluation a wholesaler is selected. There are basically three types of wholesale institutions—Merchant wholesalers, Agent wholesalers and Manufacturer's agents. The following major factors are important for the success of a wholesaler's firm—new technology, proprietary brands, niche marketing, profitability and effectiveness.

KEY TERMS

Beat plan: Beat plan or permanent journey plan is a day-level route plan made for field sales/marketing personnel to make visits to a number of stores at a predefined frequency.

Merchant wholesalers: A merchant wholesaler is an institution that buys goods from manufacturers and resells them to businesses, government agencies, other wholesalers, or retailers.

Niche marketing: A niche market is the subset of the market on which a specific product is focused.

Proprietary brands: It is a brand of product that is privately owned and controlled.

Service wholesalers: Service wholesalers usually handle larger sales volumes; they may perform a broad range of services for their customers, such as stocking inventories, operating warehouses, supplying credit, employing salespeople to assist customers, and delivering goods to customers.

EXERCISES

17.1 What are the functions performed by a wholesaler?

17.2 Describe in detail how wholesalers can be classified.

17.3 Discuss the important factors for the success of a wholesale's firm.

17.4 What are the key tasks performed by a wholesaler?

17.5 How are wholesalers different from retailers?

17.6 Write a short note on wholesaling in India.

18

Designing Channel Systems

LEARNING OBJECTIVES

LO1: To formulating the channel objectives

LO2: To learn about channel design and planning process

LO3: To identify the various factors influencing channel selection

LO4: To discuss the different methods of designing channel structure

INTRODUCTION

Formulation of channel is the first step in designing a channel system. All firms seek to achieve certain objectives by having the channel, which in turn determines the channel design the firm should adopt. Depending on the market being serviced and the nature of the product being offered, customer service is designed for an organisation. Choice from the various channel alternatives available can be made on the ease of availability of channel partners, cost of implications and ideal fit. After the marketing channels are clearly defined the process of selecting, training and keeping them motivated are all put in place.

FORMULATING THE CHANNEL OBJECTIVES

For targeted service output levels, there must be declaration of channel objectives by the marketers. Desired level of service outputs can be gained by reduction of total channel costs and coordination of functional tasks in competitive conditions. Since different service levels are required by different market segments, they can be recognised by the planners. The best channels and segments to be served are required for successful planning. With product characteristics the channel objectives are differentiated. Legal regulations, monetary conditions and competitors' channels are the various environmental factors that affect channel design.

IDENTIFYING CHANNEL FUNCTIONS

Channel functions constitute the process of maintaining flow through a channel that is performed by different members of a channel. These functions include extending credit to other channel members, engaging in after-sales services, distributing products, generating demands through selling activities, and carrying or holding inventory. Channel functions take different forms at different points of the channel.

The participation of every channel member is not required in all channel functions. The performance of certain channel functions is correlated with that of the other functions. The functions performed by the channel members cannot be substituted, however, channel members can be substituted or eliminated. For the better promotion and performance of the functions, information sharing is important.

CHANNEL DESIGN DECISION

The following situations require the need for channel decisions:

- (a) Establishing a new product line.
- (b) Making a major change in the components of marketing mix.
- (c) Aiming an existing product to new target market.
- (d) Development of new product or product line.
- (e) Facing environmental changes.
- (f) Opening new geographic marketing areas.
- (g) Dealing with changes in particular types of intermediaries.
- (h) Adapting to changes intermediary policies.
- (i) Meeting the challenge of conflict or other behavioural problems.
- (j) Review and evaluation.

CHANNEL DESIGN PROCESS

The decisions that involve in the modification of existing channels and development of new marketing channels are the decisions that refer to channel design. The process can be divided into the following six steps:

1. **The Need for Channel Design Decision:** First of all, the need is to be recognised and the organisation would require new channel for following reasons:

    ♦ When the existing channels are not suitable for the new product or product line that is developed.

♦ When the existing product is targeted to a different market.

♦ When there is a change in the marketing mix elements, when an organisation reduces it prices on certain offerings.

♦ When the legal or technological or economic environment is facing major changes.

♦ Finally, when new geographic marketing areas are opened by organisations.

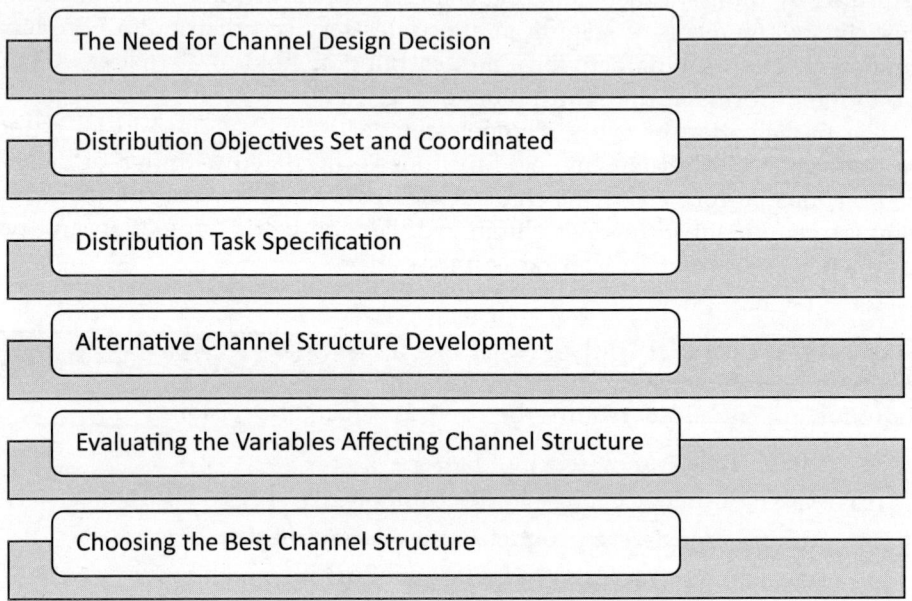

The Need for Channel Design Decision

Distribution Objectives Set and Coordinated

Distribution Task Specification

Alternative Channel Structure Development

Evaluating the Variables Affecting Channel Structure

Choosing the Best Channel Structure

Figure 18.1 Channel Design Process

2. **Distribution Objectives Set and Coordinated:** The next step for the channel manager is to develop the channel structure by modifying the existing one or developing from scratch. For well-coordinated and effective distribution objectives, the following tasks need to be performed by the channel manager:

♦ Becoming familiar with the strategies and objectives in the areas of marketing mix. In most cases, the group or the person sets the objectives of the marketing mix elements which will also set objectives for distribution as well.

♦ Setting the objectives and explicitly stating them. A good objective is one which is explicit and clear. Some examples of good distribution objectives are:

'Apple experience' is provided by Apple Computers in order to reach more customers. Coca-cola products are sold in college and school campuses to penetrate in this market.

Figure 18.2 Apple Experience

♦ Checking to see if distribution objectives are congruent with strategies and objectives of the firm. It involves verification whether the distribution objectives are not in conflict with other areas of the marketing mix or overall objectives of the company.

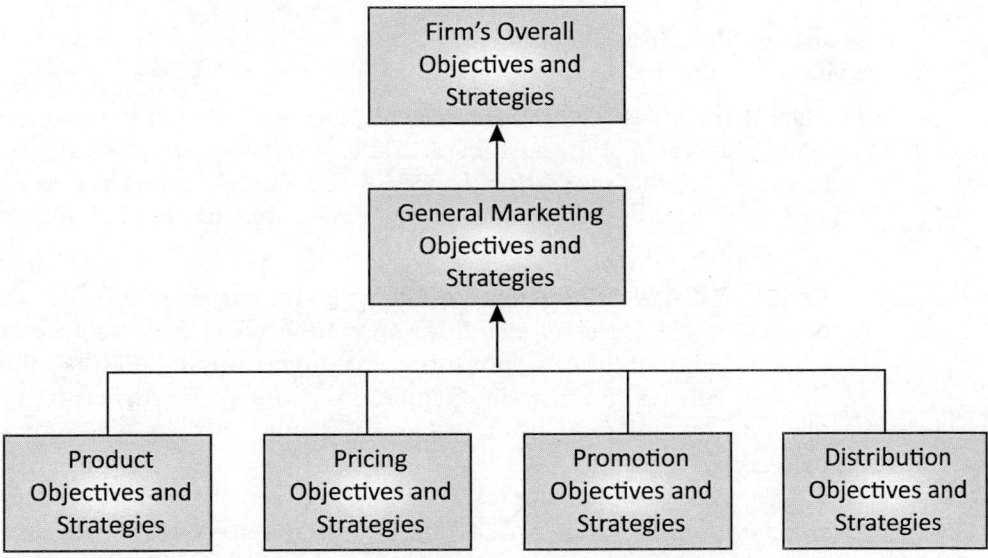

Figure 18.3 Distribution Objectives and Strategies

3. **Distribution Task Specification:** A number of tasks need to be performed after the objectives have been set. The nature of tasks to be carried out needs to be

specified by the manager. The distribution tasks include—establishing product return, providing return and service, providing warranty, arranging for credit provisions, transporting the product, processing and filling customer orders, providing hands-on experience, compiling information about the product features, timely availability, maintaining inventory, promoting product availability and target market shopping patterns. Rather than looking like distribution tasks, these functions seem to be production oriented, however, when thinking in terms of meeting customers such tasks indeed seem to be distribution tasks.

4. **Alternative Channel Structure Development:** Alternative ways of allocating the tasks should be found out once the channel manager has specified the tasks. In order to reach the customer effectively, generally more than one channel is chosen by the channel manager. For example, biscuits are sold by Britannia through pharmacies, convenience stores, departmental stores and wholesale food distributors. Despite the type of channel structure, the alternatives should be allocated in terms of (a) types of intermediaries, (b) intensity of various levels and (c) number of levels in the channel. The levels range from two to five levels. The number of intermediaries at each level specifies the intensity. The intensity is classified in the following three categories—exclusive, selective and intensive. Here, exclusive means a selective pattern of distribution. Selective means that all intermediaries at a particular level are not used. Intensive means that maximum possible outlets are used at each level.

   Firms like Rolex use a high degree of selectivity, whereas firms like Parle use a structure with intensive distribution.

5. **Evaluating the Variables Affecting Channel Structure:** The channel structure is evaluated on the basis of five categories of variables:

   ♦ *Market Variables:* The managers need to take cues from the market regarding needs and wants of the customers as the philosophy of marketing management is based on the marketing concept. The subcategories for the marketing structure include market behaviour, market density, market size and market geography.

   ♦ *Product Variables:* Many important product variables include technical vs. non-technical, degree of standardisation, unit value, perishability and bulk or weight. Bulky and heavy products have high shipping and handling costs.

   It is always good if the channel structure is short. Perishable products like flowers and food need to have a channel structure designed for rapid delivery.

   The figure explains the relationship between channel length and degree of standardisation. As the product becomes standardised it passes through many channels as compared to a simple product that passes from manufacturer to user. The maximum degree of customisation is in the B2B machinery where the product reaches industrial users from its manufacturer.

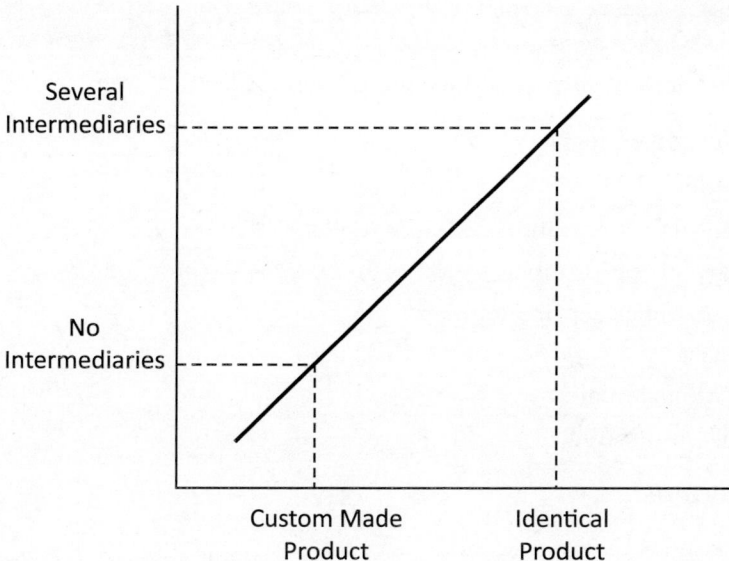

Figure 18.4 Relationship between Channel Length and Degree of Standardisation

♦ *Company Variables:* A good channel design is influenced by strategies, objectives, managerial expertise, financial capacity and size. A firm exercises a substantial amount of power if it is large in size. For financial capability also the same holds true. There is less dependency on intermediaries in case the capital available with the firm is quite large. The use of intermediaries may also be limited by the firm's strategies and objectives.

♦ *Intermediary Variables:* This includes variables like services offered, costs and availability. Availability is a key variable which influences the structure of channels. For example, Dell computers designed a direct mail order channel due to lack of a proper channel structure. Cost is another variable to be considered. If the cost of using an intermediary is high, the manager may offer to reduce the number of intermediaries. Efficient services at a low cost are provided by a good intermediary as services performed by the intermediary are an integral part of channel design.

♦ *Environmental Variables:* Different aspects of channel management and development may be influenced by macro or uncontrollable environmental forces. These include legal, technological, economic and sociocultural variables. The other variables are those on which the organisation can work upon.

6. **Choosing the Best Channel Structure:** The desired level of effectiveness offered at the lowest possible cost forms an optimal channel structure which is decided by the manager. Depending on the orientation of the firm, the channel structure is decided as there is no one set channel structure. On the basis of the data available and managerial judgement most of the channel choices can be made by the managers. (Brainskart, 2018)

FACTORS INFLUENCING CHANNEL SELECTION

The three most important factors influencing channel selection are:

Product and Market Factors

The factors include:

- Geographical concentration of the market.
- Complexity of the product.
- Level of customer service required.
- Product cost.
- Number of customers.
- Nature of the product.

Company Characteristics

These include:

- Delivering promised levels of customer service by the channel partners.
- The degree of risk to be shared by the company.
- Degree of control exercised by the company over its channels.
- Affordability of the channel and financial resources of the company.

Channel Members

These are as follows:

- Intermediaries' attitude towards policies of the company.
- Availability of middlemen.
- Level of proposed capabilities.

METHODS FOR DESIGNING CHANNEL STRUCTURE

Characteristics of Goods and Parallel Systems Approach

Aspinwall first developed this approach in the 1950s where the emphasis is on product variables for choosing a channel structure. These variables include—searching time, time of consumption, adjustment, gross margin and replacement rate. How the product characteristics affect channel structure is part of relating and describing a number of heuristics. The major problem with this approach is that for determination of channel structure it puts extra emphasis on product characteristics.

Financial Approach

This approach given by Lambert suggests that the most important variables are financial. To determine the most profitable channel, the decision involves estimating earnings on capital from different channel structures. This criterion of choosing a channel structure are more rigorous as it views the channel as a long-term investment that must cover the cost of capital invested. The problem with this approach lies in the difficulty of making it operational in decision-making context.

Transaction Cost Analysis Approach

This approach was given by Williamson and it addresses the task of choosing between channel structures with the manufacturer performing all the tasks or using vertical integration or independent intermediaries for the performance of tasks. Transaction specific assets are needed for transactions to take place. For the performance of distribution tasks both tangible and intangible assets are required. However, this method has certain limitations. Firstly, it deals with only two types of channel structure, i.e., use of independent members and vertical integration. Secondly, assuming opportunistic behaviour is not an accurate reflection of behaving in marketing channels. Thirdly, no distinction is made in short-term and long-term issues. Fourthly, operationalising the concept of asset specificity is quite difficult. Finally, TCA neglects other relevant variables, overly simplistic and one-dimensional.

Management Science Approaches

Some of the best works in this area include Atwong and Rosenbloom, Maier, Menezes, Moorthy, Rangan, Baligh, Alderson and Green, Artle and Berglund, Balderston and Hoggatt. If all possible structures could be plugged into one set of equations, then it would yield the best possible channel structure.

Judgemental Heuristic Approaches

(a) **Straight Qualitative Judgement Approach:** This is the most commonly used but the crudest approach. The evaluation of various channel structures can be made in terms of important decision factors. These factors include long-term growth potential, channel control issues, profit considerations, short run and long run costs.

(b) **Weighted Factor Score Approach**: This approach has four basic steps:

1. Explicit statement of decision factors.
2. For reflecting the relative importance in percentage terms, weights are assigned to every decision factor.
3. On a scale of 1 to 10, each decision factor is rated for the channel alternatives.
4. By multiplying the factor weight with the factor score, the overall weighted factor score is calculated for each channel.

Distribution Costing Approach

In this approach, estimation of costs and revenues for different alternatives are done and the figures are compared to find a better alternative. This approach stresses on managerial estimations and judgement based on how detailed the analysis is and what the costs and revenues of various channel structure is likely to be.

CASE STUDY

Relayware offers software and services that enable organisations to maximise and measure channel effectiveness and automate partner programs to reduce overhead, gain control and increase revenues.

The Client

Nutanix is focused on delivering IT-as-a-service, delivering invisible infrastructure for next-generation enterprise computing by natively converging compute, storage and virtualisation into a turnkey hyper-converged solution.

The Challenge

In view of Nutanix's prosperity and the business development, various sources have revealed that Nutanix is one of the quickest developing organisations in Silicon Valley.

Nutanix realises that accomplices are the way to progress and with practically its deals satisfied through the channel, Nutanix is all profoundly dedicated to its accomplices. Channel accomplices give the best insight to clients in this industry, and accomplices have been crucial for Nutanix's development procedure.

Nutanix's accomplices have solid abilities in virtualisation, VDI facilitating advances, ERP frameworks and other specialised regions. The organisation's accomplice local area unites the right blend of abilities to beneficially convey what clients need. Nutanix is focused on furnishing its accomplices with the device they need to make progress.

As channel accomplices are fundamental to Nutanix's development and achievement, the organisation needs to empower every single channel accomplice association as well as each of the employers of those associations.

Nutanix has many great worldwide accomplices, everything being equal. A few accomplices have many representatives selling Nutanix and others are a lot more modest. What's more, Nutanix needed an answer that works for each channel accomplice association paying little heed to estimate and construction.

Question

1. As Nutanix is growing at a fast pace, what kind of channel structure it must design in order to accommodate its fast-growing business?

SUMMARY

For targeted service output levels, there must be declaration of channel objectives by the marketers. Desired level of service outputs can be gained by reduction of total channel costs and coordination of functional tasks in competitive conditions. Channel functions constitute the process of maintaining flow through a channel that is performed by different members of a channel. The decisions that involve in the modification of existing channels and development of new marketing channels are the decisions that refer to channel design. The process can be divided into six steps—(1) The need for channel design decision, (2) distribution objectives set and coordinated, (3) distribution task specification, (4) alternative channel structure development, (5) evaluating the variables affecting channel structure, and (6) choosing the best channel structure.

KEY TERMS

Channel design: Channel design is the strategic process that commercial organisations use to balance resources across direct and indirect channels or routes to market.

Channel structure: A channel structure is a means of reaching your customer with your products and services.

EXERCISES

18.1 Would you use exclusive, selecting or intensive distribution for the following products:

1. Maruti Automobiles,
2. MTR Food Products,
3. Samsung Electronics?

18.2 Discuss in detail the Channel Design Process.

18.3 What is the relationship between channel length and degree of standardisation?

18.4 What are the various factors influencing channel structure?

18.5 Explain the various methods of designing channel structure.

19

Channel Management, Evaluation and Control

INTRODUCTION

Channel Management is broadly categorised into three phases:

1. Use of power bases,
2. Identification, and
3. Resolution of channel conflict and channel coordination.

POWER BASES

French and Raven identified five sources of power as follows:

Rewards: For conforming his behaviour in line with the system, the benefits given to a channel member are called rewards. For administration of marketing channels, the most popular power is reward.

Coercion: If a channel member does not fall in line with the channel requirements, then the coercive power is the hint of punishment for him.

Expertise: The special knowledge that the channel principal may have which is beneficial to the channel partners is known as expert power.

Legitimacy: The agreements or contracts provided in writing give the power of legitimacy. The parameters of behaviour expected from the signatories are clearly defined in the contracts.

Reference: Sheer association provides this kind of power. The gold standards of the industry provide this kind of power to the members associated with it.

CHANNEL CONFLICT

Channel struggle is what is going on of strife or conflict between channel individuals from the same promoting channel framework. Struggle is what is happening where one channel part sees the way of behaving of one more channel part to be obstructing the accomplishment of its objectives and its successful working.

Stages of Conflict

Conflicts occur in four stages according to the experts. These stages are as follows:

♦ **Latent:** There might be some discord among channel partners but it does not impact the achievement of customer service objectives.

♦ **Perceived:** The channel partners become aware of the opposition and the discord is clearly noticeable. These types of conflicts are also called attitudinal conflict or structural conflict.

♦ **Felt:** Here a stage of alarm, concern and worry is reached. Since the channel gets affected by the discord so it is also known as affective conflict.

♦ **Manifest:** This is the final stage of the conflict which reflects open antagonistic behaviour. The performance of the channel system is affected as open opposition is given by initiatives of the opposite party.

CHANNEL COORDINATION

Even though channel conflict persists throughout the operation of a channel system, the manager has to ensure good coordination in the channel system. A channel system is well coordinated if each channel member understands his role correctly and performs it to help the entire system to achieve its customer service objectives. In a coordinated channel the:

♦ Interests are protected for all channel members.

♦ Actions of all channel members are in line with the overall channel objectives.

♦ Channel flows are streamlined for delivering customer service objectives as per end customer's desires.

CONFLICT MANAGEMENT

For managing conflicts four steps need to be taken as under:

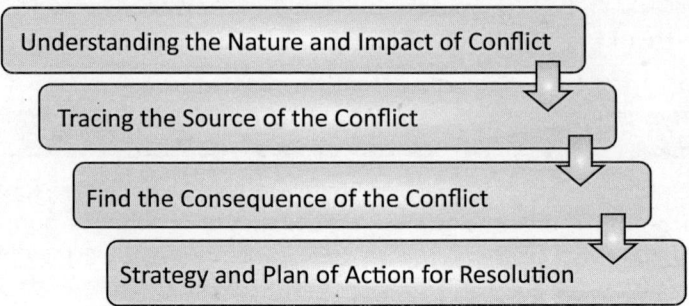

Figure 19.1   Stages of Conflict Management

1. **Understanding the Nature and Impact of Conflict:** This step deals with identification of the conflict and understanding the seriousness of the conflict. Further stages in this step include:

   ◆ Listing the major issues that could be a source of concern between the parties involved. These issues could be related to settlement of claims, credit extension, coverage and infrastructure provided by the distributor.

   ◆ Some of these issues may be routine and may not be serious. Therefore, it is required to rank the issues according to importance.

   ◆ All issues may not arise at the same frequency and at the same time. So, it is necessary to check the frequency of occurrence of these issues.

   ◆ The next step is to assess the expectations and perceptions about the issue.

   ◆ The last step inventories the frequency of occurrence, ranking of importance and views of the parties concerned on what really seems to be the problem.

2. **Tracing the Source of Conflict:** Broadly the causes of conflict can be identified as:

   ◆ *Clash of Goals:* This is the most common problem. The distributor may have the goal of maximizing profitability whereas the principal objective might be hundred per cent market coverage.

   ◆ *Different Perceptions:* The perception of channel members may vary regarding the competition, customers, product features and role in channel system.

   ◆ *Unclear Domain:* The third problem is related to unclear definitions of the domain. Some members may feel that others are not pulling the weight of achievement of channel objectives.

   ◆ *Market Domain Conflicts:* Such conflicts could arise between:
     − Channels outside the system.
     − Channel members at different levels in the same system.
     − Channel principal and the channel partners.
     − Similar channel members in the same system.

3. **Consequences of Conflict:** When a conflict escalates into a dispute there is "distrust" in the system. This mistrust and discontent may further give way to other problems.

4. **Strategy and Plan for Resolution:** Some ways of managing conflict are:

   ◆ Collective goal setting is a way of dealing with conflict which can be mutually agreed upon.

   ◆ Extending participation in the planning process to the channel partners. So, they are more likely to abide by the decisions which they feel they have made.

   ◆ As part of the training process, the trainees can be made to work in the business of the channel partners. This helps in the creation of confidence in the channel members.

   ◆ Last resort is arbitration, mediation by third party and diplomacy.

SCOPE OF CONTROL

The scope of control is quite wide. It covers all the areas of business including marketing, inventory, finance and production. Control may be financial or physical. Physical control may be qualitative or quantitative. Control is influenced by checking or supervision.

STANDARDS OF PERFORMANCE

The performance results of the individual are judged or measured against a standard. The following characteristics should be possessed by a standard:

◆ With a reasonable amount of time and effort one should be able to achieve a standard.

◆ Rather than procedures, a standard should concentrate on the results.

◆ There should be flexibility in standards.

◆ As per the objective of the organisation, a standard should be set.

◆ Monetary or physical terms should be used to express standards.

SYSTEMS CONCEPT AND MANAGEMENT

For conversion of disorganised resources into effective and useful enterprise there is a requirement of money, machines and men. Input, sub-system and output are the three basic elements of a system. A system may be classified as a structured or semi-structured system.

System Mission

A mission is usually product oriented or market oriented. In order to define the mission, the firm defines the desired system output and associated costs.

Mission: Product "Alpha" serves All India Market with 98% delivery within 5 days at the lowest possible cost.

CONTROLLING THE DISTRIBUTOR

A distributor is a "firm or organisation which acts as the company's sole selling agent in a particular area which is known as his territory". A distributor remits money to the company, collects payment, maintains stock of company's products and redistributes them in his area.

Salesperson's job at the distributor's place:

- Checking stock level of material with the distributor.
- Standing by commitments and being fair in dealings.
- Always keeping the paperwork updated.
- Always maintaining friendly relations with the distributor and listening carefully to their suggestions.
- Never accepting money from the distributors or accepting favours.
- Ensure the distributor redistributes the goods within 24 hours in the same town.
- Ensuring that any scheme for retailers always reaches them 100% interest.
- Ensuring the distributor maintains a separate stock registers for the range of products.
- Ensuring that the distributor maintains stocks by rotation.
- Ensuring that the distributor maintains 45 days stock of the products.
- Ensuring that the distributor opens shop at the proper time for avoiding loss of market hours.

CONTROLLING THE RETAILER

Retailing is of utmost importance in the entire process of selling. A retail shop is a place where consumers who are actual users, buy products in units. Products are selected by retailers for their shelves on the basis of the following:

- Regular availability
- Retailer's margin
- Product's packaging
- Product's shelf-life
- Product quality
- Product's reputation among consumers
- Products awareness

Jobs Done at Retail Shop

♦ The salesperson should make the retailer aware of his presence as soon as he enters a retail shop.

♦ The salesperson should utilise the precious time to shop, when retailer is busy with customers. Following observations can be made:

  (i) Stock pressure of competitor's products in the shop.

  (ii) To assess the potential of the shop, total stock pressure of all products can be made.

  (iii) Location of stocks of salesman's interest; easily located near the customers and ideal location of product stocks.

  (iv) Checking competitor's material as well as noting down new material being introduced and new products being launched. Also, noting customer's response, stock pressure, packs and pricing.

  (v) The product's stock pressure should be noted on regular visits and finding out reasons for poor/good sale; the order to be placed by the shopkeeper is mentally outlined.

♦ Salesperson should introduce himself properly when he finds the shopkeeper free for interaction

♦ The salesperson should greet the retailer and leave the shop after booking the orders.

Objections Held by Retailers

♦ Replacement not provided instantly.

♦ Incomplete range.

♦ High damage during transit.

♦ Local brand is provided in place of reputed brands.

♦ Proper painting not available in shop.

♦ Credit of the distributor is squeezed up.

TOOLS FOR CONTROL

For the purpose of controlling channel members, there are two conventional methods:

1. **Contract:** One of the most commonly used and oldest tools for control in Indian context is the contract.

2. **Power:** For controlling the channels of distribution, another tool that is available is power.

KINDS OF CONTROL DEVICES

Control of devices are divided into three categories:

1. **Reports and Budgets:** The most frequently and most obvious used control devices are budgets and reports. An established reporting system brings information monthly, weekly and daily basis.
2. **Dealer Relations Index:** Measuring the overall effectiveness of the distribution programme requires this quantitative technique.
3. **Distribution Audit:** The comprehensive and systematic analysis of all activities and results of a distribution programme form part of distribution audit.

DISTRIBUTION COST CONTROL

One of the basic functions of marketing is distribution. The job of marketing remains incomplete until the product reaches the door of consumers for ultimate consumption or use. A significant and increasing part of many companies' expenditure is in keeping their products on the move through distribution channels to ultimate consumers. Physical distribution covers a wide variety of activities concerned with administration, inventory control, packaging, material handling, warehousing and transportation. It is at those points in the distribution flow where the products stop moving that they accumulate costs.

Analysis and Control of Distribution Costs

Increase in sales may result when high level customer service is provided. This may be done by providing speedy delivery or increasing the proportion of sales outlets. However, the marginal benefits from a product may be reduced when cost of dispatching small quantities of products that are dispersed geographically is exceeded.

Method of Fixing a Budget for Distribution Expenses

The cost data should clearly be classified into its basic characteristics whether the costs are variable or fixed. The actual cost incurred should be mentioned before distribution function starts its plan for the planning period in question.

CASE STUDY

Favourite Snacks Ltd. is a company which makes staple branded food products like maida flour, suji and wheat flour along with ready to eat foods, all under the brand name, Favourite. The 'Favourite' is very strong in one region of the country.

It is a family-owned company but strongly believes in professional management. However, it still clings on to traditional methods of management. This is mainly because the top management feels these methods have been time tested and proven. FSL has its headquarters in one of the secondary towns and not in a major or metro city. It also has one of its three plants in this location. The location of the other two plants is also in regions where FSL is strong.

FSL has a good network of dealers in the region and many dealers have been with the company for many years and support the products of the company with a good distribution effort in the marketplace.

FSL is run by a CEO and a COO. It has general managers heading R&D, purchase, IT, supply chain, finance, marketing and production. Most of these general managers have MBA as their qualification.

FSL does not pay high salaries as compared to the industry but is able to so far retain its people because the top management is quite benevolent and treats its people well. In recent times, a number of local big players and even MNCs are entering the industry and offering astronomical salaries to good people. In particular, marketing and sales people of FSL are very well recognised in the industry as an excellent resource for strengthening and keeping a high distribution presence for the products entrusted to them.

One of the major competitors of FSL with an all India presence, was also rapidly expanding its sales and marketing network and started looking for good sales and marketing people in the industry. Obviously FSL was the first place they started looking at. In recent times, this major competitor took away the GM-marketing of FSL with a higher package. Once the earlier GM-marketing of FSL joined the competing firm, he started the process of "poaching" good salespeople from FSL to build his sales team.

FSL promoted a senior sales manager with high experience and good performance to his credit as the GM-marketing for PFL.

FSL has a serious dilemma on its hands:

♦ It is losing all its efficient marketing and salespeople to FSL which is offering huge salary packages which FSL cannot match.

♦ Even though FSL allows its people at Head Office to commute from one or two major cities nearby, the location of FSL is not attractive to the top talent of the industry.

♦ FSL cannot easily recruit new, experienced salespeople from the outside as many of its competitors have increased the salary levels which cannot be matched by FSL.

♦ FSL is worried that it will be left with salespeople not having a ready market in the industry.

Meanwhile, the business has to go on. FSL has also got to demonstrate to its 500 odd dealers in the region that it is still a market leader and can take care of its manpower issues efficiently. The industry is also watching the moves which FSL makes.

Questions

1. If you are the new GM-Marketing of FSL, what action will you take as the GM-Marketing to build and protect your valuable team.
2. What action will you take to keep your dealers highly motivated and performing in spite of changes in sales management?

SUMMARY

The scope of control is quite wide. It covers all the areas of business including marketing, inventory, finance and production. Control may be financial or physical. Physical control may be qualitative or quantitative. Control is influenced by checking or supervision. A distributor is a "firm or organisation which acts as the company's sole selling agent in a particular area which is known as his territory". A distributor remits money to the company, collects payment, maintains stock of company's products and redistributes them in his area. Retailing is of utmost importance in the entire process of selling. A retail shop is a place where consumers who are actual users, buy products in units. One of the basic functions of marketing is distribution. The job of marketing remains incomplete until the product reaches the door of consumers for ultimate consumption or use. A significant and increasing part of many companies' expenditure is to keep their products on the move through distribution channels to ultimate consumers.

KEY TERMS

Cost control: Cost control is the practice of identifying and reducing business expenses to increase profits, and it starts with the budgeting process.

Channel conflict: Channel conflict occurs when manufacturers disintermediate their channel partners, such as distributors, retailers, dealers, and sales representatives, by selling their products directly to consumers through general marketing methods and/or over the Internet.

Distribution: Distribution is the process of making a product or service available for the consumer or business user who needs it.

EXERCISES

19.1 Explain in detail the channel management.

19.2 Discuss the control issues in a channel system.

19.3 What are the criteria that can be used to evaluate channel members?

19.4 What are the strategic and functional implications of control of channels?

19.5 How can channel profitability analysis aid in the management of distribution channels?

20

Digital Supply Networks

LEARNING OBJECTIVES

LO1: To understand the digital supply networks

LO2: To discuss the transport intelligence and logistics system

LO3: To identify the short-term risk management strategies

LO4: To identify the long-term risk management strategies

INTRODUCTION

The Covid–19 pandemic has shown that the majority of the companies are not prepared to bear shocks which has exposed their vulnerability. In order to drive up asset utilisation, reduce inventories and minimise costs; most companies removed flexibility and buffers to absorb any disruptions.

With the advent of new supply chain technologies, it has been possible to change this scenario by making improvement in end-to-end supply chain visibility. This may help companies to resist shock and create support for the companies.

Digital Supply Networks (DSN) have evolved from the traditional supply chain model. The functional silos are broken down and enable optimisation, agility, collaboration and end-to-end visibility by making the organisations connected to the entire supply network. DSN were designed in such a way so that they may make use of technologies like 5G, robotics, artificial intelligence and Internet of Things.

Organisations applying DNS are ready to deal with the unexpected whether it may be supplier bankruptcy, sudden spikes in demand, labour dispute, regulatory change, act of war or terrorism, trade war or the most recent Covid–19 (Kilpatrick and Barter, 2020).

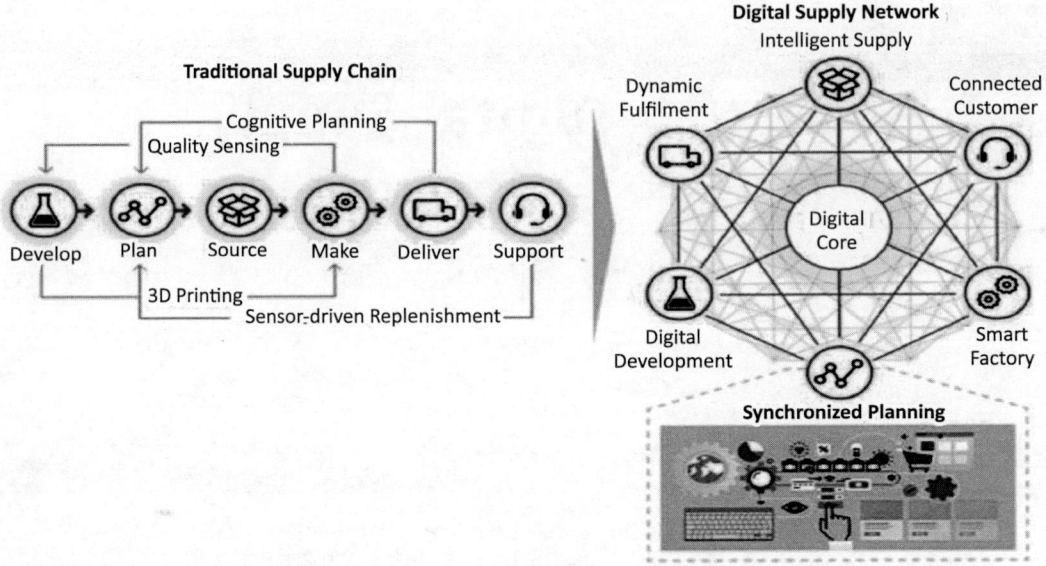

Figure 20.1   Shift from Traditional to Digital Supply Network
(*Source:* Acungil, 2019)

Organisations applying DNS are ready to deal with the unexpected whether it may be supplier bankruptcy, sudden spikes in demand, labour dispute, regulatory change, act of war or terrorism, trade war or the most recent Covid–19 (Kilpatrick and Barter, 2020).

How Companies Mitigate the Impact?

♦ **Companies Mitigating the Impact:** The companies who were better prepared to mitigate the impact were the ones who developed business continuity strategies and implemented supply chain risk management. In order to reduce risks pertaining to any particular region or country such companies diversify their supply chains. To prepare for supply chain disruptions such companies undertook inventory strategy. To reduce the dependency on any one supplier, the strategic components and commodities were multi-sourced.

♦ **Companies Responding to Uncertain Events:** In order to drive specific actions based on their priorities and to better understand the risks of an extended supply chain network, these companies have put systems in place so that strong relationships can be built.

♦ **Companies that are Scrambling:** These companies rely heavily on single supplier or a single geographical area for key products. They can not see the risks because they do not have enough visibility across the extended networks. Their systems are weak and are not able to understand the project stock-outs of finished products or direct materials, optimise production and inflexible logistics networks ensuring flow of goods.

TRANSPORT INTELLIGENCE AND LOGISTICS SYSTEMS

Before the pandemic, Indian organisations had totally lean and interconnected supply chains. The chains increased the efficiency of the system by ameliorating the gaps. However, extreme supply chain disruptions (SCD) were exposed unveiling the supply chain vulnerabilities. These supply chain disruptions mainly include problem in custom clearance, shutting down of ports, limited mobility, reduced freight capacity, time delays and impact on transportation and logistics data. International trade was restricted and it added fuel to the fire in logistics sector. The mobility of goods was sharply reduced due to restrictions on transport freight. Restrictions due to lockdown have brought intermodal and first- and last-mile transportation have come to a complete halt. Both domestic and external trade have been impacted substantially; these restrictions have caused equipment shortages and reduction in vessel capacity.

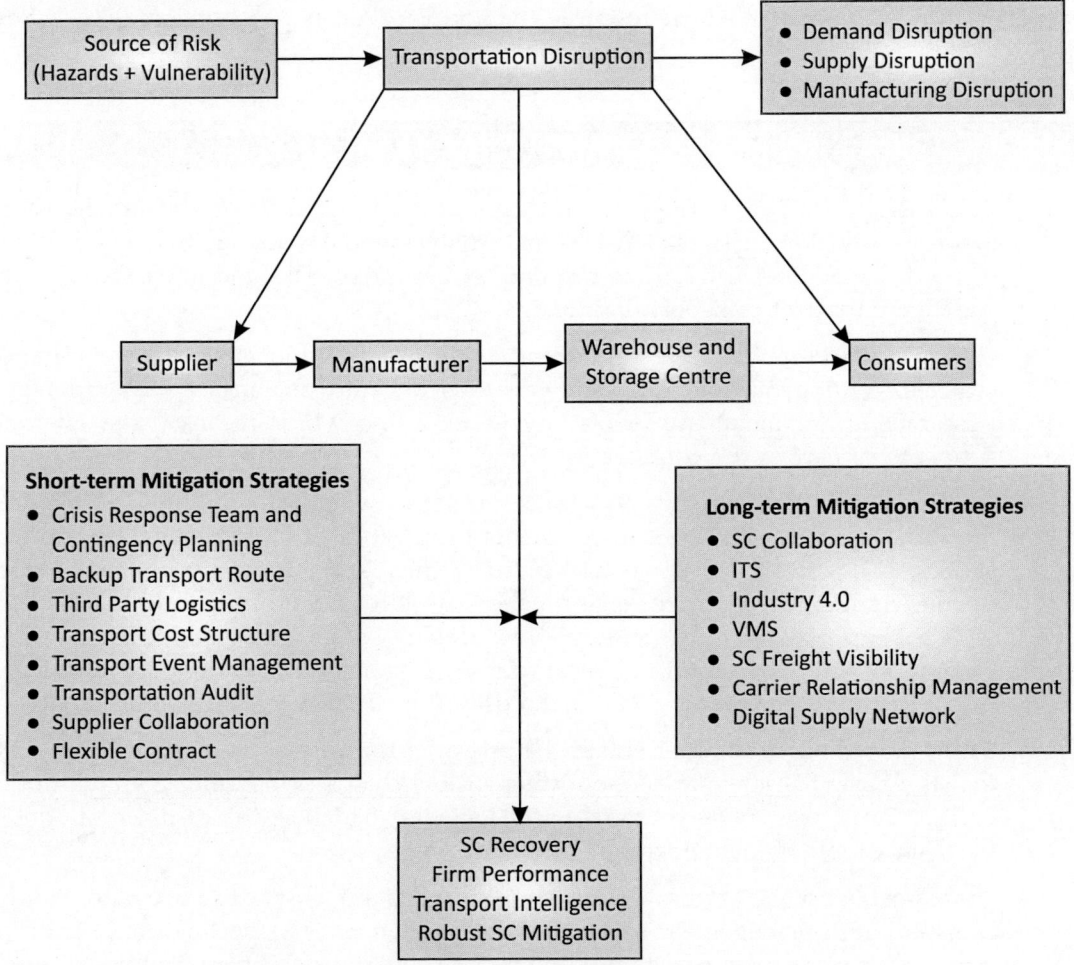

Figure 20.2 Transportation Risk Management Model
(*Source:* Sudan and Taggar, 2021)

Due to pandemic induced restrictions, the aviation sector was the hardest hit. All passenger flights were suspended and only cargo flights were allowed. This is significantly impacted logistics and transportation performance in achieving predicted future potential.

Robust response was required to mitigate the disruptions induced in logistics and transportation systems due to Covid–19. One of the responses at the pre-pandemic level could be complete revival of ports and shipping. The domestic market has been linked with the global market with the strong participation from shipping sector.

The lack of sound mitigation strategies and inadequate technology interventions has caused a backward movement leading to a negative growth. There has been a decline by 20 per cent in the domestic road transport sector.

Despite lack of modern technological intervention and severe transportation disruptions, the sector that has achieved significant growth during the pandemic is the e-commerce sector. In order to help the continuity of their businesses and to mitigate delivery delays, e-commerce players sought alternative warehousing locations. The demand for online sales was boosted as e-commerce players followed the norms of social distancing and contactless delivery.

SHORT-TERM RISK MANAGEMENT STRATEGIES

- ♦ **Crisis Response Team:** The planning gaps in the transportation system should be identified by the crisis response team. Analysing the vulnerability analysis and response capabilities can help to respond to disruption risks and understanding the negative impact of transport disruptions.

- ♦ **Contingency Planning:** Due to disruptions in external and internal transportation systems, contingency planning should focus on auto products and components. Researchers also make use of contingent rerouting which means using alternate suppliers as part of the contingency plan.

- ♦ **Backup Route:** The logistics and transportation diversification strategies required the firms to make significant investments in advance of any potential disruptions similar to Covid–19. The direct and indirect transportation costs must be absorbed by the companies on occurrence of a disruption and these must be associated with backup supply route strategy. This strategy should integrate occurrence of a disruption with expenditure of resources. Analogously, if the standard mode gets disrupted then the company can make use of emergency transportation mode.

- ♦ **Third-party Logistics:** Firms should be prepared for unforeseen events. Third party logistics have the potential of supporting supply chains at the time when disruption occurs. Effort was made by third party logistics to reduce the distance of contact between suppliers, manufacturers and consumers.

- ♦ **Transport Cost Structure:** Firms should focus on cost structure and routine transportation management to survive the pandemic. Transportation cost involves two aspects—production costs and unit costs. There is instability in the transportation network because of carrier rates and unit costs. Productivity costs form part of the opportunity cost during disruptions.

◆ **Transport Event Management and Outsourcing:** Hour-to-hour focus on waste reduction and identification and daily event management should be targeted. Problem solving techniques like generating real-time metrics, completing a real-time track, creating daily route designs can be used after detecting any waste. If transport outsourcing is required then it must also be reported.

◆ **Transportation Audit:** Transportation audit across all geographies and modes should be targeted through a comprehensive implementation. By identifying the opportunities upstream in the areas of sourcing, planning and execution areas. Transportation audit can be performed for transportation procedures, shipping needs and reviewing carriers.

◆ **Supplier Collaboration and Flexible Contract:** Various domestic suppliers need strong cooperation and collaboration. Firms should have a relationship with backup suppliers. On the occurrence of transportation disruption, such relationships help gain advantage over competitors and reduce the impact of disruption.

LONG-TERM RISK MANAGEMENT STRATEGIES

◆ **Supply Chain Collaboration:** The warehousing activities, transport and continuity of flow are the logistics processes that work in collaboration. Several B2B and B2C were facilitated for achieving reduction in costs. Robust cooperation was demanded for strong collaboration between information technology, customers, suppliers and firms.

◆ **Intelligent Transportation System (ITS):** With strong application of information technology firms can implement their transportation systems efficiently and effectively. The interconnection of different systems for capturing, communicating, computing and assisting the decisions with proper management. Some of the widely used applications for ITS include Emergency Vehicle Pre-emption (EVP), Transit Signal Priority (TSP), Vehicle Data Collection (VDC), Traffic Management Systems (TMS), Highway Data Collection (HDC) and Electronic Toll Collection (ETC).

◆ **Industry 4.0:** Firms should adopt and integrate transportation and logistics systems with industry 4.0 to form logistics 4.0. Logistics 4.0 is the combination of applications and innovations added by the cyber-physical system. Logistics 4.0 must rely on application of information security, intelligent transportation system, transportation management system, warehouse management systems and resource planning. Resilience in supply chains have helped firms to strengthen redundancy, agility and flexibility.

◆ **Vendor Management System:** Wal-mart and other retailers have used a successful business model like vendor-managed inventory. VMI increases collaboration between retailers, distributors, manufacturers and suppliers. Transportation disruptions that are caused by the supply and demand disruptions can be analysed through this.

◆ **Supply Chain Freight Visibility:** Information related to supply chain freight operations is called supply chain freight visibility. IoT sensor technology has been crucial for tracking shipments. Through the use of cloud services, the tracking of equipment, vehicles and inventory can be done.

♦ **Carrier Relationship Management:** When carriers, providers and shippers came together to form a dedicated team balancing performance and cost. Each player comes at odds with the others clutching, blaming and arguing at their positions.

♦ **Digital Supply Network:** In today's volatile marketplace, firms lack the agility and end-to-end view of supply chain. DSN refered to transportation networks and information linked digitally. Various problems in the supply chain can be solved by DSN which include insufficient risk management, conflicting priorities, poor response times and lack of visibility. Characteristics required for building a DSN include: connected, intelligent, scalable and rapid. Replacing the traditional chain with DSN enhances integration of information, financial, physical and talent for promoting open communications and collaboration with downstream and upstream suppliers (Sudan and Taggar, 2021).

CASE STUDY

The Changing Supply Chain of Amazon

The innovative technologies deployed by Amazon and bold use of supply chain strategies by them have changed the face of retail. Its competitors are struggling to catch up as it is reshaping the supply chain continually.

Phase of Rapid Growth

After 10 years since it was founded, in 2004 Amazon annual revenue was around $7 billion. By 2018, it had reached $ 233 billion. It became the fastest company which only took 20 years to reach $ 100 billion. It has been growing at 20% since its inception. It is believed that the company is aiming at $ 1 trillion and aims to reach this goal by 2027. Thus, it can be said that the transformation of Amazon from a bookseller to a formidable force in the retail industry is praiseworthy. The continuous effort made by Amazon for fast delivery of its products puts immense pressure on its competitors to perform well.

Strategy that Changed the Game for Amazon

When Amazon launched Amazon Prime in 2005, customers received delivery within two-day by paying for annual membership. This proved to be a game changer which helped Amazon establish dominance over other retailers. When the competitors started providing the same two-day service, Amazon shocked everyone with the one-hour delivery option. Thus, its innovative strategies have always proved to be profitable for the business.

Advanced Practices

Due to its quick and efficient supply chain, Amazon enjoys a cult following. What makes Amazon efficient is the excellent transportation, multi-tier inventory management, extensive network of warehouses and sophisticated information technology.

1. **Insourcing Logistics and Outsourcing Inventory:** The infrequently ordered products are not stored in the regular warehouses and the majority of its inventory is outsourced. Fifty per cent of the Amazon sales are done by third party sellers. However, for fast

deliveries it uses its own delivery systems instead of third-party sellers because involving them would lengthen the process.

2. **Delivery Options:** Amazon has different options for different services like free super saver delivery, first-class delivery, one-day delivery and prime delivery. Taking care of every customer's preference for delivery makes it a logistics expert.

3. **Push-Pull Strategy:** The strategic placement of its Amazon's warehouses helps keep them stocked. They are also located close to city centers and metropolitan areas for convenience.

4. **Zones:** The number, size and location of the warehouses proves to be an important factor. There are five kinds of storage areas: random storage for smaller items, reserve storage for low-demand items, case-flow storage for high-demand items, library storage stores books and pallet prime storage.

5. **Automation:** Kiva Systems, a robotic and automated warehouse solution was acquired by Amazon in 2012. This company was renamed as Amazon Robotics in 2015. The warehouse activities can be completed quickly with the assistance of Amazon Robotics. Amazon has 45,000 warehouse robots as of 2020.

6. **Cost of Supply Chain:** Amazon has been able to keep its per unit supply cost to a minimum due to large economies of scale. As a result, it has been difficult for other companies to compete (Leblanc, 2020).

Questions

1. How can competitors match the innovative supply chain practices of Amazon?
2. How can Amazon improve its digital streaming service?
3. How can Amazon increase ad revenues from merchant sellers?

SUMMARY

Digital Supply Networks (DSN) have evolved from the traditional supply chain model. Organisations applying DNS are ready to deal with the unexpected whether it may be supplier bankruptcy, sudden spikes in demand, labour dispute, regulatory change, act of war or terrorism, trade war or the most recent Covid–19. There are three ways in which companies mitigate the impact: mitigate the impact, respond to uncertain events and companies scrambling. There are short term and long-term strategies for managing risk. The short-term risk management strategies include: crisis response team, contingency planning, backup route, third-party logistics, transport cost structure, transport event management and outsourcing, transportation audit and supplier collaboration and flexible contract. The long-term risk management strategies include: supply chain collaboration, intelligent transportation system, industry 4.0, vendor management system, supply chain freight visibility, carrier relationship management and digital supply network.

KEY TERMS

Digital supply network: Digital Supply Networks establish a "digital thread" through physical and digital channels, connecting information, goods, and services in powerful ways.

Intelligent transportation system: An intelligent transportation system (ITS) is an advanced application which aims to provide innovative services relating to different modes of transport and traffic management and enable users to be better informed and make safer, more coordinated, and 'smarter' use of transport networks.

Supply chain disruption: A supply chain disruption is a breakdown in the manufacture flow of goods and their delivery to customers.

EXERCISES

20.1 What is a Digital Supply Network? Explain its importance.

20.2 Why is there a requirement of Intelligent Transportation System?

20.3 Explain the short-term risk management strategies.

20.4 Briefly describe the long-term risk management strategies.

21

Logistics and Supply Chain Management

LEARNING OBJECTIVES

LO1: To understand the concepts of logistics and supply chain management

LO2: To describe the principles and systems of inventory management, warehousing management and transportation management

LO3: To review the various modes of transportation

LO4: To discuss how IT enables logistics function and learn about the use of technology in logistics function

INTRODUCTION

The "reach" for a service or product is provided to the customers through marketing channels. The "physical" distribution efforts should be able to support the reach and thus be handled by the Logistics and Supply Chain functions. The space and time utilities of the marketing channel system are supported by logistics and supply chain management. Like other functions, supply chain and logistics functions get their cost effectiveness and performance measured by specific methods on delivering customer service. Information technology has added value to the supply chain and logistics functions by providing tools for analysis of information and enhancement of customer service capabilities.

DEFINITIONS OF LOGISTICS

The procurement, maintenance, distribution and replacement of personnel and materials.
—Webster Dictionary

The science of planning, organizing and managing activities that provide goods or services.
—Logistics World

The processes of planning, implementing and controlling the efficient, effective flow of goods, services and related information from the point of origin to the point of consumption for the purpose of conforming to customer requirements.

—Council of Logistics Management

Scope of Logistics

A wide range of service and manufacturing organisations can be encompassed under logistics. It can include:

♦ Choice of operation in markets.

♦ Choice of management of carriers, selection and mode of transport.

♦ Management and location of storage facilities.

♦ Building up of distribution network.

♦ Policies for customer service.

♦ Cost and service levels as part of inventory management.

♦ Decision on layout and location of plant.

♦ Impact on storage and transportation using packaging decisions.

MATERIALS HANDLING

Managing inventory includes the function of handling materials. The activities under materials handling include:

♦ **Reception, Storage and Dispatch of Goods:** It can be reception of packing materials and raw materials from vendors, storing of finished goods and raw materials and dispatching of finished goods to the distribution channels.

♦ **Order Packing and Picking:** Based on customer's orders a "picking" list is prepared by the warehouse personnel. Picking may be manual or by using handling equipment like forklift. Packing refers to aggregation of all materials under single order. Order picking can also be related to components or items issued by stores for meeting indentations from shop floor production.

♦ **Goods Sorting:** Whenever an assortment of truckload of goods are received, there is a sorting done before sorting them in appropriate manner.

♦ Repacking which is part of additional processing where damages to the original packing are done. Only after repair do the goods get dispatched.

♦ Arranging loading and transport of goods on to the truck or whatever required mode dispatch of goods is there till selling points.

Inbound vs. Outbound Logistics

1. Inbound or upstream logistics include reception, storage and issuance of inputs that take care of:
   - Materials handling.
   - Inventory control.
   - Inbound quality inspection.
   - Scheduling of production to manage "issues".
   - Return of unacceptable materials back to suppliers.
2. Outbound or downstream logistics include distribution, dispatch, storage and collection of finished goods to consumers/buyers/distribution channels include:
   - Shipping and related documentation.
   - Delivery of vehicle operations and scheduling.
   - Warehousing in the field and the plant.
   - Materials handling of the finished goods.
   - Order processing of all orders received through sales system.

SUPPLY CHAIN MANAGEMENT

The process of planning, implementing and controlling the efficient, cost-effective flow and storage of raw materials, finished goods and related information from the point of origin to the point of consumption for the purpose of conforming to customer requirements. —Council of Logistics Management

Factors Influencing Supply Chain

An innovative Supply Chain:

- Provides consistent excellent service to the customer by executing and planning in a synchronised manner.
- Enhances the speed. Companies can not only meet delivery dates and commit but also take care of requirements in emergency.
- Maximises possession, place and time utilities for improving service levels.
- Helps in reducing costs of operation. As the saying goes "companies do not any longer compete with each other. It is the supply chain of companies which compete with each other".
- Meets all customer driven challenges in terms of delivery, quality and best price as specified by the customer.

DIFFERENCE BETWEEN SUPPLY CHAIN MANAGEMENT AND LOGISTICS

Pete Crosby's Viewpoint

Logistics includes transportation, warehousing, distribution and customer service physically. Supply chain includes logistics business function including material management, inventory control, production scheduling, manufacturing operations besides those mentioned above.

Logistics Consultant's Viewpoint

Functions of supply and logistics can overlap. Generally, logistics is concerned with coordination and strategy of flows between production and marketing. A supply chain tends to focus on procurement and purchase. It may include production planning, inventory and materials.

Council of Logistics Management's Viewpoint

As per the Council of Logistics Management: "Logistics Management activities typically include inbound and outbound transportation management, fleet management, warehousing, materials handling, order fulfilment, logistics network design, inventory management of third-party logistics services providers. To varying degrees, the logistics function also includes sourcing and procurement, production planning and scheduling, packaging and assembly, and customer service. It is involved in all levels of planning and execution—strategic, operational and tactical. Logistics Management is an integrating function, which coordinates and optimises all logistics activities, as well as integrates logistics activities with other functions including marketing, sales, manufacturing, finance and information technology."

"Supply chain Management is an integrating function with primary responsibility for linking major business functions and business processes within and across companies into a cohesive and high performing operation."

Jeff Ashcroft's Viewpoint

Supply chain management is looking at active management of the whole enchilada whereas logistics can relate to parts within the supply chain. Sometimes the two terms are used interchangeably, others feel there are some differences.

FOCUS AREAS OF LOGISTICS AND SUPPLY CHAIN MANAGEMENT

There are three main focus areas which include inventory management, warehousing and transportation.

1. Inventory management
2. Warehousing
3. Transportation

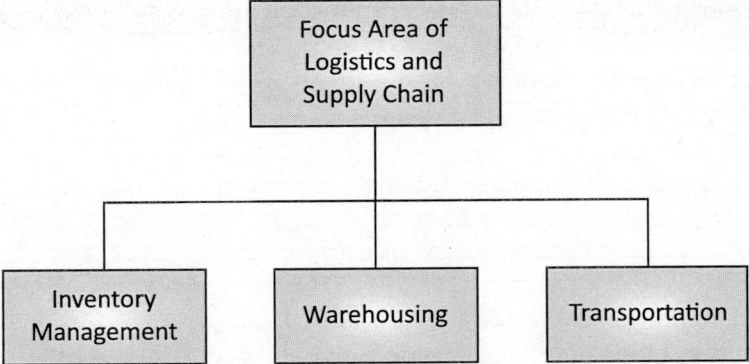

Figure 21.1 Focus Areas of Logistics and Supply Chain

INVENTORY MANAGEMENT

The inventory management objectives include:

- **To Maximise Customer Service:** Inventory holdings ensure availability of stocks when and where required. Inventory is a protection against any kind of uncertainty. For example, if a competitor is not able to service the market with his products for any reason, the company should have enough inventories to fill the gap in the market.

- **To Minimise in the Cost of Plant Operations:** Production can happen in economic batches. If production has to get these economies, it has to pack lot sizes of different SKU as per schedule and build up stocks.

- **To Minimise Holding Cost:** Minimum investment to deliver the agreed customer service.

Functions of Inventory

It acts as a buffer between:

- Demand and Supply: In terms of quantities and the timing.
- Finished Goods and Customer Demand: In terms of quantities and the timing of the demand.
- Requirements for an operation and the output from the previous operation on the shop floor.
- Parts and materials to begin an operation and suppliers of the materials.

Reasons for Carrying Inventory

- **WIP:** Production rates, which depend on men and machines, are finite and well defined. Production also requires a number of steps to be completed and each stage may take varying amounts of time.

- ◆ **Cycle Stock:** This is again on the production line to minimise set-up costs and times which are fixed.
- ◆ **Seasonal Stock:** The resources for production like machines, manpower is fixed but the demand can be seasonal. There is a need to build up finished goods stocks.
- ◆ **Safety Stock:** Demand is a random variable and uncertainties of supply cannot always be foreseen; some level of safety stock is always maintained.

Warehousing

Warehouse is a building where large quantities of goods are stored before being sent to shops. The place utility part of logistics is provided by warehousing or storage. The desired level of customer service which is promised at the lowest possible total cost is the major purpose of warehousing. The warehousing is that part of logistics of a company that includes item storage and is located between the point of consumption and the point of origin.

Reasons for Warehousing

The reasons for warehousing:

- ◆ The materials that need to be disposed of or recycled are provided temporary storage.
- ◆ Provision of the right mix of products at all locations and at all times to the customers.
- ◆ According to the relevance in the automobile industry, providing support to JIT programs with customers and suppliers.
- ◆ Overcoming space and time differentials—not possible to have production units closer to markets.
- ◆ For a desired level of customer service ensuring the least logistics cost.
- ◆ Support for sudden changes in demand and change in market conditions.
- ◆ When prices are favourable then forward buying and taking advantage of purchase discounts offered.
- ◆ Dispatching full truck loads to distribution centers for achieving transportation economies.
- ◆ In terms of set-up times achievement of production economies.
- ◆ Uninterrupted maintenance of supply sources for storage of safety stocks near markets.
- ◆ Customer service policy being supported by the company.

Distribution Warehousing

There are three ways in which location strategies for warehouses can be defined:

1. **Market Positioned:** In this case warehouses are located closer to the customers. This location is influenced by factors such as:

- ◆ Level of service offered for customers
- ◆ Size of the orders
- ◆ Product sensitivity
- ◆ Cost of transportation
- ◆ Cycle time of order

2. **Production Positioned:** In this case warehouses are located closer to the facility of production. Here the level of service may be lower than the market positioned alternative. Factors which influence the location are:

- ◆ Consolidation rates of transportation
- ◆ Ordering of assortments from mix of products
- ◆ Number of products in the product mix
- ◆ Raw materials perishability

3. **Intermediately Positioned:** In this case warehouses are located in between the producer and the final customer. Even when products are made in a number of units still a high level of service is possible.

Size of Warehouse

Factors that help in determining the size of the warehouse include pattern of demand, aisle sizes, office space, stock layout, materials handling system, economies of scale, size of product portfolios, production lead times, size of markets served, throughout rates and stock norms.

DIFFERENT MODES OF TRANSPORT IN INDIA

There are several modes of transportation in the existing transport system. These include air, road, rail, and shipping.

Railways: The principal mode of transportation in India is railways. People from all corners are brought together with the help of this. During the past century Indian Railways has proved to be a great integrating force. There has been phenomenal growth in the Indian Railways system. It has played a vital role in the social, industrial and economic development of the country. The network is divided into 9 zones which are further sub-divided into divisions. The basic operating units are the divisions. The Indian railways has four gauges that is broad gauge, metre gauge, narrow gauge and standard gauge. The main objective of railway planning was to develop the infrastructure of transportation. Besides the major thrust areas, there has been rehabilitation of assets, upgradation of standards and technological changes in important areas like areas of track, signalling, wagon bogie designs, passenger coaches and locomotives.

There are mainly five undertakings under the Ministry of Railways (i) Konkan Railway Corporation Limited, (ii) Container Corporation of India Limited, (iii) Indian Railways

Finance Corporation Limited, (iv) Indian Railways Construction Company Limited, and (v) Rail India Technical and Economic Services Limited. The research and development wing of Indian Railways is known as the Research, Design and Standards Organisation.

Characteristics	Rail	Road	Pipeline	Air	Water
Door to door service	Sometimes	Yes	Sometimes	No	Sometimes
Price	Low	High	Very low	Very hight	Very low
Speed	Slow	Medium	Slow	Very high	Low
Reliability	Medium	Medium	Very high	Very high	High
Packaging needs	High	Medium	Nil	High	High
Risk of loss/damage	Medium	Medium	Very low	Low	Medium
Flexibility	Low	High	Very low	Very low	Low
Environmental impact	Low	Medium	Low*	High	Low

*Possibility of disaster causing significant impact.

Figure 21.2 Characteristics of Various Modes of Transportation

The new marketing strategies have the following features:

(i) Container Corporation of India Limited provides international transport, transportation in bulk for small customers and door to door services to domestic customers.

(ii) Leasing out brake van space to customers so that they may have assured transportation between fixed points.

(iii) Simplification of rules in key areas like faxing of invoices, single window booking system supply of wagons and free acceptance of indents.

(iv) In the empty flow direction, there will be a rebate of freight for utilisation of wagons.

(v) For facilitating faster movement there needs to be closure of yards.

Roads: One of the largest road networks is found in India. The seventh five-year plan laid emphasis on coordinated coverage of state highways, secondary and feeder systems as well as rural roads.

♦ *National Highways:* The responsibility of the national highway system is with the Central Government. Though national highways carry 40% of the road traffic, they constitute only 2% of the road length.

♦ *State Highways:* It is the responsibility of the State Governments to maintain the state highways and the district rural roads. The development of certain selected roads is also under the preview of the state government.

Major Initiatives for Highway Development

For the development and maintenance of national highways, a separate ordinance has been promulgated by the government for land acquisition.

The government has also levied a toll on completed 4-lane sections which may be funded through the budget.

The National Highway Authority has permitted the participation of the private sector for the promotion of equity in the private or public sector.

Shipping: Overseas shipping has an important role in India's trade. There are a large number of shipping companies available in India. Coastal shipping is an energy efficient and comparatively cheaper mode of transport.

Inland Water Transport

In India, there is a vast network of waterways including creeks, backwaters, canals and rivers which is 14,500 km in length. Besides the organised operations by mechanised vessels, there is high use of country boats in various canals and rivers.

National Highways

The government identified ten important waterways that may be considered as National Waterways. The Ganga between Haldia and Allahabad, Udyogmandal Canal, Champakara Canal, Kollam-Kottapuram stretch of West Coast Canal, Saidya-Dhubri stretch of the Brahmaputra.

IT ENABLING THE LOGISTICS FUNCTION

Speed is the essence of customer service as has been realised by many companies. Customer service can be improved if companies can react faster to customer needs using IT enabled processes. Broadly, there are four recognisat drivers of supply chain which include facilities, inventory, transportation and information technology. Here, the role of IT is critical as activities of the other three are coordinated with the help of IT services.

Information is a key driver of supply chains. In a multi-product company, the information has to be processed in large numbers for which IT enabled operations are required.

Electronic Data Interchange (EDI)

EDI is defined as the exchange of business information through standard interfaces by using computers.

— Ministry of Finance, GOI

EDI has benefits such as time, saving inventory, lower processing and handling costs, improved availability of information, faster, far better accuracy and reduced paperwork.

Bar Codes

The most cost-effective, popular and common way of tracking items is bar codes. These are observed on packaging as a series of vertical lines which can be scanned using a bar code reader for identification of items. Bar code is an item identifier representing alphanumeric identification of desired parameters. Some uses of bar codes include:

- Faster and better-quality control of selected items.
- Usage on production lines for identification of products made in various shifts.
- Inventory picking at a store.
- Inventory tracking in the stores.
- Incoming material receipt in a plant.

Radio Frequency Identification (RFID)

This is an improvement over the bar-coding method. It has the ability of tracking equipment, people and items while being in line of sight. RFID technology consists of a serial number which transmits information wirelessly. Electromagnetic pulse is continuously sent out through the transmitter. The information is automatically read and registered. Two types of tags used are: (i) read only and write (ii) active and passive.

CASE STUDY

Jasch Ltd. is a well-established manufacturer of spun yarn. It has a good reputation for service and quality. The company decided to expand its operation through exports because of the expanding global market. The company formed a team of Materials and Marketing department to study the possibilities of global logistics. An extensive study was conducted for the same and it was found that domestic and global logistics are mostly the same:

- Safety and economic regulations exist.
- Processes like vendor payment, procurement, carrier selection, order processing, warehousing and inventory management are required.
- Information is critical for cost control, management of inventory and customer service
- Both systems involved storage and movement of products.
- The framework of linking customers, plants and supply sources is the same.

The transportation system of the company was reliable and economical. For exports as well they decided to evaluate capabilities of their existing transporter and entrusted them with the job of transport till port. For customs formalities a contract was agreed upon with the company's agent for shipping.

The response was excellent for the company and it could get as many as 20 customers in three months and reached a level of USD 300,000 per month by the end of 6 months. Based on this response the volume of exports was expected to grow to USD 500,000 per month in a year. When the review was made at the year-end it was found that the volume of exports came down to USD 120000 which was much lower.

An emergency meeting was held to discuss and the exports manager was told to identify the reasons for the decrease in exports volume. So, he decided that visiting customers would be best for information. On receiving feedback from customers, it was found that even though the price and quality were good, customers were upset with losses due to transit, improper identifications, changes in shipping schedules and delayed shipments.

So, he checked the dispatch schedules and found that production and work schedules were proper. Then he studied the logistics systems and found that it costs very high. The motivation level of logistics people was low due to lack of coordination, disorganisation and overwork.

Questions

1. What logistics model should the company go for ensuring proper operations of the company?
2. Explain the problems experienced by Jasch Ltd. What is the main reason behind these problems?

SUMMARY

The processes of planning, implementing and controlling the efficient, effective flow of goods, services and related information from the point of origin to the point of consumption for the purpose of conforming to customer requirements. A wide range of service and manufacturing organisations can be encompassed under logistics. The process of planning, implementing and controlling the efficient, cost-effective flow and storage of raw materials, finished goods and related information from the point of origin to the point of consumption for the purpose of conforming to customer requirements. There are three main focus areas which include inventory management, warehousing and transportation. The place utility part of logistics is provided by warehousing or storage. There are several modes of transportation in the existing transport system. These include air, road, rail, and shipping. Speed is the essence of customer service as has been realised by many companies. Customers service can be improved if companies can react faster to customer needs using IT enabled processes. Broadly, there are four recognisat drivers of supply chain which include facilities, inventory, transportation and information technology.

KEY TERMS

Inventory: Inventory or stock refers to the goods and materials that a business holds for the ultimate goal of resale, production or utilisation.

Logistics: The procurement, maintenance, distribution and replacement of personnel and materials.

Supply chain: The process of planning, implementing and controlling the efficient, cost-effective flow and storage of raw materials, finished goods and related information from the point of origin to the point of consumption for the purpose of conforming to customer requirements.

EXERCISES

21.1 What do you understand by logistics management? Define its scope and objectives.

21.2 What are the major functions of a warehouse? How is warehousing related to inventory decisions?

21.3 Explain briefly the difference between logistics and supply chain management.

21.4 Enumerate the benefits of using technology in supply chain management.

21.5 What is the influence of information technology on the other three supply chain drivers?

21.6 Explain the various modes of transport in India.

21.7 What are the strategies followed by railways in India?

References

Acungil, S.E. (2019). Blockchain Enhanced Supply Chain. Istanbul Technical University.

Cofano, A. and Scarpi, D. (2020). Unieuro: Retail Management in a Global Crisis. Retrieved from https://www.bbs.unibo.eu/research/unieuro-retail-management-in-a-global-crisis/

ETCIO. (2021). Salesforce aligns equality with benefits offered to employees Retrieved from: https://cio.economictimes.indiatimes.com/news/corporate-news/salesforce-aligns-equality-with-benefits-offered-to-employees/88449510

Gupta, S.L. (2002). *Sales and Distribution Management.* Excel Books, New Delhi.

Havaldar, K.K. and Cavale, V.M. (2006). *Sales and Distribution Management: Text and Cases,* Tata McGraw-Hill Education, New Delhi.

Jain, S. (n.d.). Theories of Selling—Traditional and Modern. Lecture Notes.

Khan, M. (2005). *Sales and Distribution Management.* Excel Books, New Delhi.

Kilpatrick, J., and Barter, L. (2020). COVID–19: Managing Supply Chain Risk and Disruption. *Deloitte: Toronto, ON, Canada.*

Lang, S. (2020). 3 Examples of Highly Successful Sales Training Programs. Retrieved from https://elearningindustry.com/examples-of-highly-successful-sales-training-programs

Leblanc, R. (2020). How Amazon is Changing Supply Chain Management, Retrieved from https://www.thebalancesmb.com/how-amazon-is-changing-supply-chain-management-4155324

Oluwabamidele, P. (2009). Modern Approach to Marketing Management. Retrieved from https://oluwabamidele.blogspot.com/2009/09/personal-selling.html.

Panda, T.K. and Sahadev, S. (2005). *Sales and Distribution Management.* Oxford University Press, New Delhi.

Still, R.R., Cundiff, E.W. and Govoni, N.A.P. (1988). *Sales Management.* Pearson Education, New Delhi.

Sudan, T., and Taggar, R. (2021). Recovering Supply Chain Disruptions in Post-COVID–19 Pandemic Through Transport Intelligence and Logistics Systems: India's Experiences and Policy Options. *Frontiers in Future Transportation, 2, 7,* pp. 1–8.

Index